Below: *Washington Dulles control tower.*

Major Airports
of the World

Major Airports of the World

Roy Allen

LONDON
IAN ALLAN LTD

First published 1979

ISBN 0 7110 0918 X

© Ian Allan Ltd 1979

Published by Ian Allan Ltd, Shepperton, Surrey;
and printed in the United Kingdom by
Ian Allan Printing Ltd

Note: runways are identified by their magnetic
bearing on the compass and abbreviated — hence
Runway 28 has a magnetic bearing of 280° ±5°.
The bearing is always related to the direction of
operation, while the letters L and R signify left and
right.

BRAATHENS S·A·F·E

OLAV KYRRE

Contents

Previous page, top: *Designed as a replacement airport for the old airport at Torslanda, Gothenburg's new airport at Landvetter opened for service in November 1977.*

Previous page, bottom: *Landside view of Gothenburg's new airport, at Landvetter.*

Left: *Only rural airports or airports with moderate apron activity can allow this type of uncontrolled straggling today, which may be amusing for young flyers but which can be hazardous.*

Introduction

When Ian Allan Limited kindly invited me to write *Major Airports of the World*, a follow up to my original *Great Airports of the World*, first published in 1964, I was interested for a number of reasons, not the least of which was that, in the 11 years since the second edition, I had personally been to very many more airports, all over the globe, and developed an excellent and, I hope, mutually beneficial relationship with the men who manage them and their planners, who continue to offer interesting concepts to the world at large in the face of new uncertainties.

The changing operational climate was another reason for looking afresh at the airport scene with this book, for in a decade the climate has totally changed, from pointing to a future with apparently limitless growth to one where financial constraints, a new preoccupation with energy sources, and air transport's most worrying recent phenomenon — terrorism — now shape the thinking of planners and airport authorities the world over, and markedly influence international airport development.

In recording facts about some 70 of the world's major airports it was sobering, therefore, to be aware that had we not had an oil crisis a third London airport would be under construction now, with similar projects, such as Saltholm and New York's fourth international airport, given the impetus they previously would have received as routine; that a

continuance of inflation levels 'enjoyed' by most of the world 10 years ago would have seen even greater, uninterrupted, growth rates in air transport, with a consequent impression made upon airport design, probably to provide for greater numbers of supersonic airliners; and that a world free from hijackers and saboteurs, as aviation once was, did not require the construction of 'coup-proof' airports nor armies of security guards, which are now natural design provisos.

The world airport scene is today, however, busier than ever in spite of the recent troubles that have beset civil aviation, and is no less interesting because of such important shaping factors. Airport authorities have shown, as they have extended generous help to me, that expansion is still the order of the day, if perhaps in new directions, with new goals in mind, and that the airport industry certainly has a great future.

The following pages bear this out, and it is encouraging also to report upon developments which reflect what might be called the airport industry's new maturity. As an example of this, Britain is now conducting courses in airport management training which will ensure a steady supply of future airport administrators as well as controllers. Carried on by the British Airports Authority and the Air Transport & Travel Industry Training Board, these courses represent a new contribution by Britain for UK and overseas airports. Two or three years ago there was nothing like them on offer.

To my friends in the world airport industry I record my sincere thanks for their interest in this new book and their help with facts, statistics and photographs. To those authorities who preferred not to assist, for 'security' or other reasons, I say why not think again, next time around?

Roy Allen

Below: *The Seadrome concept was proposed for Maplin and the model shows the action of floating breakwater protection for the runways. Note the road and rail link.*

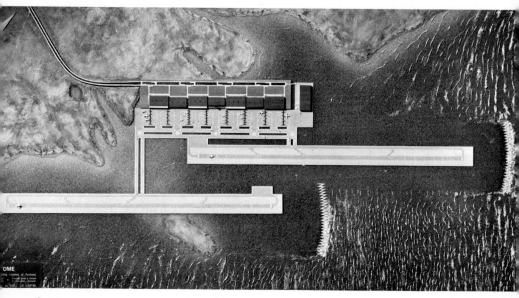

OME

6

Part One

Airport Types and their Location

As the photographs in this book show, the airports of the world have come a very long way from the grass fields with a few simple markers which characterised the start of air transport 60 years ago. Indeed, the international airport business has become an exact science, bringing into play a whole range of disciplines and equipments including electronics, mechanical systems, audio and visual communications, traffic management, transport planning and fuel handling, as well as Customs procedures, cargo processing and 'people-moving'. The airport terminal, and its related buildings, is the hub of all this activity, and in thinking of airports we naturally tend to think of this as the airport itself.

By way of establishing the various types of airport in use around the world, however, it is instructive to classify them and look at the various categories they fall under. This has nothing to do with terminal design or runway layout, which are planning matters, but, rather, airport types, of which there are a number.

They include the all-grass, the land-based and the water-based airports of which the latter is similar to but not the same as the offshore type. Variations of these include the grass and concrete airport, that is, the grass airfield equipped with one or more concrete runway, the all-concrete airport, and the floating airport, which has been an interesting concept of recent years.

These airports will fall into different categories which indicate their operational function, such as regional, major international, general aviation and satellite etc. The term is not generally used in Britain but in the USA there are 'hub' airports and these are classified as large, medium and small according to the number of communities the airports serve: a non-hub airport is one which sees the embarkation annually of less than 0.05% of the national total of airline passengers.

There are charter airports and transit airports, although neither of these are specific categories but have come to be so classed because of the nature of their operations. The charter airport, for example, has come to be known by this term because the bulk of its traffic is inclusive tour or charter traffic and its facilities are geared to this type of operation (as Luton, for example, in the UK). Likewise, the transit airport is not a specific class, but it will be found in many countries handling a preponderance of transit traffic. In this regard it is interesting to know that Athens Airport was rated in 1975 by the Hellenic Civil Aviation Authority as the busiest transit airport among 36 of the world's international airports, the explanation being that Athens serves as a connecting point for so many international flights. Equally, Athens is a busy scheduled-traffic airport.

The regional airport serves, as it suggests, various regions with the bulk of its traffic, while the satellite airport is one which serves as a feeder airport to the nearby major facility, often a principal international hub, such as New York's John F. Kennedy International Airport. The satellite airport often serves as an 'overflow' and diversion airport for the

Below: *Frankfurt is a good example of the major international airport, a land-based, purpose-built concrete facility handling over 56,000 passengers a day. In terms of traffic, Frankfurt is the eleventh busiest passenger airport in the world and ranks fourth in cargo tonnage handled annually.*

main international facility, from which it is sometimes found expedient to divert flights because of weather problems or traffic congestion. The British Government, incidentally, recently proposed four new categories of airport in England and Wales with its new master plan for the development of the nation's airports up to 1990. These were: Gateway international airports; Regional airports, to serve as a second tier and catering mainly for UK domestic, international short-haul and charter services; Local airports, which would cater mainly for local needs; and General aviation airports, a type of facility well known in some countries like the USA, but which has been almost non-existent up to now in Britain.

There are heliports and seaplane bases, particularly in the USA, where in 28 states there are some 620, many offering channel navigational lights and fuelling, restaurant and other facilities. The heliport is licensed for helicopter operations and is in a class of its own insofar as it excludes fixed-wing aircraft. There are few purpose-built heliports in the United Kingdom, but this number is likely to grow as private business flying increases yearly and the prospect of international services by public carriers using helicopters becomes a real probability.

Airline operations do not take place on any scale from all-grass airports, but there are some of these airfields still endearing themselves to the hearts of visitors, notably in the UK, where new civil operators continue to launch themselves into business in spite of the odds against them. Pleasant country fields, such as Sywell Airport, Northamptonshire, play their part in making these starts possible at relatively little cost.

In distinct contrast and becoming known as the most promising types for the future are the water-based airports, which have their runways and a portion of their terminal facilities built adjoining or actually over water. A large number of this type of airport has been proposed in recent years, among them the now defunct Maplin project, which would have been partly built on land reclaimed from the sea, and the most recent Changi Airport, Singapore, which is actually well ahead in construction as this book is being written. These provide for massive passenger terminal complexes and long runway systems to handle international traffic. As land becomes scarce and expensive the coastal or water-based airport has much to offer, for it has environmental attractions too, with minimum aircraft noise and little pollution. Sydney, Honolulu, Changi, Kiushu in Japan, Haugesund in Norway, Rio de Janeiro and Nice are all airport locations on or adjoining the sea developed in the last few years.

Taking this concept a stage further, although without much progress so far, is the true island airport, which is literally planned as a floating offshore airport. This type has been proposed as a completely man-made structure, anchored some way off the coast from the city the airport is intended to serve, and bearing runways, passenger terminals and all administration blocks. The island airport is linked to the land by a causeway, which would carry a high speed train service for passengers and personnel.

If one adds to all of these the much talked of all-cargo airport, which is sometimes regarded as attractive but generally agreed to be a commercial non-starter, the number of categories and types of airport is seen as substantial. There may even be more in the future.

Below: *The massive growth of scheduled and non-scheduled cargo traffic in the past few years has led to the frequent cry for the creation of all-cargo airports. Several have been proposed but they are generally regarded as commercially impracticable, largely because half of the current air cargo traffic is carried in the belly holds of passenger airliners.*

Airport Design

While the different types of airport in use stem largely from air transport evolution, airport design has been given close attention in the past 25 years and in the past 15 it has become something of a scientific study.

Everybody knew — or thought they knew — when hard runway airports began to be built that operators required at least one runway facing into wind, and another for operations in the next most likely wind direction. This thinking was followed by a period which saw multi-runway patterns, appearing to take care of all such problems; then aircraft weights and performances became such as to make runway numbers and bearing strengths practically immaterial, with only the runway length appearing to matter. It is interesting in this regard to listen to the arguments about Gatwick Airport today, where, for largely environmental reasons, its operators maintain that it will never need a second runway to handle the traffic that is proposed for it. Just 20 years ago, in 1958, when it was re-built to a Stage 2 development plan, land was earmarked for a second, parallel runway at Gatwick as a matter of course, as plans show, with the only uncertainty about this runway being the precise date when it would be required.

Considerations over runway arrangement today have changed as aircraft have become more advanced, and design has come to be centred upon operational requirements, with new factors playing a part. Thus, an airport built to have more than one runway will most likely be designed with a view to multiple take-offs and landings, and the runways therefore arranged in parallel. Dallas/Fort Worth Airport and Narita, Tokyo, are typical examples of this thinking, with the American airport not even really having to bother about the other prime factor which influences airport design today — noise.

This has become a planning matter, with airport authorities in constant debate with aircraft constructors as they try to resolve air transport's requirements for the future. The quieter aircraft that are coming, however, will be joined by shorter take-off and landing aircraft, and this will have its effect upon airport design. With future transport aircraft runway lengths common today could be halved, and a new and safer era of operations begin.

In looking at airport design today, planners consider in particular operational requirements and the economic aspect of the whole facility, and consequently design characteristics derive from these. While the airport is still something of a showplace, its parallel runway system will have been incorporated in order to maximise the number of take-offs and landings during a working year and thereby get the best value from what is a very expensive undertaking. Likewise, the actual lengths of runways laid down will have been dictated by the runway requirements of contemporary aircraft, and up until recently these have been 10,000ft and more (two of the runways at Dallas/Fort Worth are 11,400ft long).

The demand for such incredible amounts of runway space imposed strains upon localities which became too much to bear in certain places, among them London and New York which were both glad to find unnecessary the need to construct additional international airports when forecasts signified a slowing down in growth. When a third London airport has to be built it will be interesting to see how aircraft performance has changed its specification.

Below: *Gatwick Airport, in its 1958 form, with single pier terminal and single runway. Land for the second runway, on the right, is now built over.*

In looking at terminal design, planners are caught today between creating attractive, and sometimes grandiose, structures and purely functional facilities where a prime consideration is handling an impressive annual traffic throughput. In this difficult task they generally do a good job, for there are so many factors to take into account now as it is recognised, finally, that air travel is just one element in an integrated transport system, rather than being a special means of moving about the world.

With airport terminal design the planner has to look at passenger throughput at peak times and provide enough space to allow for large numbers of passengers. Equally, he has to consider the off-peak periods and the amount of money under-utilised space can cost authorities. As an example, the first stage passenger terminal at Narita Airport will handle a maximum of 3,200 departing and arriving passengers an hour in the peak periods, which had to be equated with terminal costs; in total, Narita cost $793 million.

Then again, the planner has to consider the place of the airport in the total traffic scene. Is it intended to be, for example, a replacement airport for a city, as Charles de Gaulle Airport was for Le Bourget? With such knowledge in mind the planners of the

Paris Airport Authority were aware that Roissy had to be large, capable of substantial expansion up to the end of the century, and equipped with the most modern systems of transporting travellers while on the ground and between their aeroplanes — the reason for which they were there in the first place. Equally, the PAA planners knew that, as the airport for the capital city of France, Charles de Gaulle Airport had to be astride main road and rail arteries. In its finished, unlovely rough-concrete form, CDG Airport may not be attractive to the visitor, but it does fulfil its role.

The terminal design at Roissy represents one approach to handling the passenger. Travellers are separated and channelled according to their flight to one of seven satellite terminals surrounding a main structure ('the Aerogare'). This satellite concept had been employed previously at Toronto and Geneva, and elsewhere. At Toronto for a variety of reasons it failed, while at Geneva it has been a success. Other airports, such as London's Heathrow, employ other design ideas, such as taking the traveller up one or more levels above the ground in his passage through the terminal, and then back down to the ground on the airside in order for him to board the aircraft.

If such planning ideas do not work or seem poor ideas, they have to be numbered among the many considerations requiring much thought, including baggage handling and flow, private car movement and accommodation, provision for invalids, large numbers of buses, delayed aircraft, with their prospect of parties of passengers, and the provision for airport and airline administrational functions and, perhaps, the most important matter of all, eating and drinking.

Below: *The finger-and-gate system of channelling passengers was first modified by the covered walkway, a simple design improvement in the terminal area.*

Running the Airport

Inevitably, airport administration has become more bureaucratic over the years, but this is not a criticism; rather it is a comment upon the remarkable development of a system which could not be left to untrained managers and demanded the professional touch of highly qualified men and organisations to cover every aspect.

There are not many airports about the world now that handle commercial air services without some degree of governmental involvement, for if an airport is privately owned it will almost certainly have ATC services provided by a government body, and it is more than likely that government finance will be provided to help run the airport. An airport handling air carrier services is part of a system which now stretches around the world, and for this reason local and central government bodies have become involved and various airport professional organisations tied in.

Airport ownership and administration is readily classified. Air transport airports are owned by local authorities, such as municipalities, towns or states, by the government of the country in which they are located, or by autonomous operating bodies which have been established by the government and local authorities between them or by the government alone: relatively few are privately owned.

In the United Kingdom a number of the regional airports are owned by local councils or authorities — typical examples are Manchester, Luton, Liverpool and Birmingham. East Midlands Airport is owned by an authority made up of the Derbyshire, Leicestershire and Nottingham county councils. The matching arrangement in the USA might be typified by Baltimore-Washington Airport, which is owned by the State of Maryland.

Government-owned airports are the most common, and in Britain these are represented by the airports operated by the British Airports Authority, which was established by the Government under an Act of Parliament as an autonomous owning and operating body. The BAA is otherwise a nationalised concern, responsible to the Government. In other parts of the world, ranging from the Middle East to Africa and South America, the state is the sole owner and operator of airports in particular countries.

A development in more recent years, which is seen increasingly, is the BAA-type of autonomous owner/operator. This type of undertaking can be found in India, where the IAAI is responsible for the major gateways of Bombay, Delhi, Calcutta and Madras; in Denmark, in the form of the Copenhagen Airports Authority, and in Holland, where the Amsterdam Airport Authority is responsible for Schiphol. There are many more, and a recently established Authority has been that for Curacao Airport, in the Netherlands Antilles, which has been created to free the airport from direct government operation.

At Schiphol, however, as at Frankfurt and Cologne, the state is a partner in the ownership of the airport rather than its sole controller, for the airport authority has been established as a company and, in the case of Amsterdam's airport, the shareholders in this company are the State of the Netherlands, the Municipality of Amsterdam and the Municipality of Rotterdam. Flughafen Frankfurt AG has principal shareholders in the Federal German Government, the State of Hesse, and the city of Frankfurt am Main. Likewise Cologne-Bonn Airport operates as a company, whose principal shareholder is the Federal Republic which shares responsibility wih the Land of North Rhine-Westphalia and the city of Cologne.

The running of the world's airports is often the province of organisations other than the state or the appointed airport authority, for this is a specialised task, and one in which Britain has been particularly skilled. In overseas locations such as the Middle East and Africa it is quite common, therefore, to find airports in states such as Dubai and Abu Dhabi, in the United Arab Emirates, and Swaziland under the management of British companies like International Aeradio, whose services and skills have probably ranged from supplying and installing the air traffic control consoles and related equipment, to providing ATC and management personnel to handle the complete tasks of administration. At Southall, Middlesex, the headquarters of IAL conducts training courses for the nationals of these countries to ultimately assume responsibility for the airport operational tasks.

In the planning of airports, government bodies play a central role today, as might be expected, for there are so many issues which require the overseeing of government departments, such as surface transport infrastructure, environmental disturbance and, of course, safety. There are also the matters of international telecommunications and the airways system, and the government must have final authority over these. Because the whole airport system is now so complex, however, various specialised organisations and bodies with special skills have come to make important contributions to the industry, and these range from the airport divisions of associations such as ICAO and IATA to the 'trouble-shooting' councils such as ICAA, AOCI and the WEAA.

These last are essentially airport associations, whose members meet regularly to discuss developments of mutual interest and report on various ideas, such as with the Paris-based International Civil Airports Association and the Washington-based Airport Operators Council International. Such bodies are often the medium through which airport-users' interests are made known and effected to the betterment of air transport generally and for the users in particular — which include goverment planners and administrators as well as the airlines and general passengers at large.

Passenger Facilities and Amenities

One of the reasons why air travel has taken over from surface transport as the means by which people travel today is its simple attraction of being advanced in every respect. In Victorian times, when railway travel was a brand new experience, the equipment and facilities were doubtless breath-taking to the travellers of the time, and in the supersonic era air transport is similarly awe-inspiring, pleasureable, and remarkable in its achievement for the passenger.

The airport is the hub of the operation, and it might be said to be the railway terminal of the jet age, for as air transport continues to move forward at a steady pace, enlargements and further improvements to existing facilities are made, and these in turn seem to attract yet more traffic.

There is no doubt whatever that the aircraft and the airports have been greatly responsible for the fantastic volumes of traffic that are moved today, for as a result of the constantly made improvements the international airport has generally become a comfortable and entertaining place, as well as one holding tremendous interest and excitement. Where else, for example, can one always find a great number of people of different nationalities gathered together except at the airport? Where else can one have a fine meal and be given an aerial show at the same time but at the airport restaurant? For the person interested in languages, aeroplanes, technical devices and ideas, foreign countries and pretty girls, the airport is probably the best place in the land.

The true commercialisation of airport services occurred first in the home of air transport, the USA, when it was recognised that the provision of a variety of attractions could bring in more money than that required solely to provide for the passengers. With the monies from concessions and a variety of rents, the operating authorities gained revenue to help pay for their airports and fund development schemes, and in due course this became the accepted routine.

From such moves the world has gained a whole range of airport services, from the snack bars to a range of restaurants, airport hotels, motels, cinemas, hairdressing facilities, florists, sauna baths and showers, banks, hire car services, bookstalls and gift shops, airport museums, spectators' galleries, and, of course, the duty-free shop. All of these facilities are in the best interests of travellers and have done much to swell the numbers of people flying, although it might be thought that things have reached a curious state when 50% of the British Airports Authority's revenue now comes from rents and such concessions, and without such income the seven BA airports would have made a substantial overall loss in 1976-77.

It must be acknowledged that the BAA has been a leader in the provision of some services for passengers at its airports, however, among them lifts, inclined ramps and special toilets for disabled travellers, and first-aid rooms and medical services, as well as restrooms for mothers with small children.

Moving walkways are now features of most big airports, and these devices, sometimes called travelators, Speedwalks or moving pavements, take a lot of the effort out of reaching the holding lounges disposed around or at the end of the piers. The one criticism that might be made of these is that they are rarely long enough and far too few in number.

Below: *Many airport authorities have come to recognise that airports are exciting places for people who may travel very little. Airport shops are therefore important facilities for travellers.*

Right: *For the airport authorities, the duty-free store has become a crucial source of revenue, and vast sums of money are now turned over in these curious international marketplaces, which may be said to function solely because of outdated regulations.*

Below right: *Island check-in counters are employed in Terminal 1 at Heathrow to provide numerous and uncluttered facilities for passengers on United Kingdom and some European flights. Some idea of the great size of this terminal is evident from the picture.*

Above: *Airport signposting has become an art, requiring the best skills of graphic designers to get the message across to travellers of different nationalities.*

Centre left: *The holding lounge came into use proper with the wide-bodied jets, and with the large capacities of these aircraft is now a necessary feature of major airports. This one is at Heathrow.*

Bottom left: *The moving walkway was introduced first in North America when the piers in the finger and gate system became longer. Now common at major airports across the world, these conveyors take a lot of the effort out of walking to the holding lounge or gate while carrying bags. They can usually be varied in speed, according to traffic.*

Top: *As much a convenience and aid to the passenger as it is to the airport authority, the passenger loading bridge, known in this instance as Aviobridge, has been one of the best ideas to be introduced at international airports. Apart from providing a direct link for the passenger to the aircraft cabin from the terminal, it avoids the use of the airside bus, which in spite of its need to be scrapped remains in large-scale use by various authorities.*

Above: *British Airways has its own fleet of buses in use at Heathrow for passenger transfer operations. For the traveller, such vehicles, however new and well-driven, generally provide an uncomfortable start or finish to their air journey. Invariably overcrowded, they also involve the passenger being exposed to the weather between the vehicle and the aircraft.*

Arrivals flight	from	last stop	due	expected	landed	information
SA 223	JOHANNESBURG		06:30	06:35		
BA 931	SYDNEY	BAHRAIN	06:35	19:00		DELAYED TIL 14TH
MS 779	CAIRO	ZURICH	14:25		14:35	BAGGAGE IN HALL
AC 865	ZURICH		14:35		14:25	
AR 132	BUENOS AIRES	PARIS	14:55		14:50	BAGGAGE IN HALL
BA 811	DELHI	BEIRUT	15:20	15:50		
TW 701	FRANKFURT		15:40			
GF 009	MUSCAT	BEIRUT	16:10	15:30		
PK 781	KARACHI	PARIS	16:20	16:35		
ME 203	BEIRUT		17:00			
PA 001	DELHI	FRANKFURT	17:35			
ET 706	ADDIS ABABA	ATHENS	17:45			

Passengers ending their journey in this terminal normally leave the Customs Hall approximately 30 minutes after the time of landing

As airports get busier some facilities are introduced to answer a need while others, regrettably, disappear because of new pressures or fresh thinking. Heathrow saw the opening of an underground rail link in December 1977, which now makes it possible for passengers to journey right through from Piccadilly Circus to the heart of the airport with their baggage and without changing trains, and this service is expected to be used by a substantial proportion of the airport's users before long. While nothing to to with the airport authority, the check-in facility at the West London Air Terminal was closed beforehand, thus denying passengers the chance of disposing of their baggage to the airlines before reaching the congested halls and check-in counters of Heathrow. For the many travellers who use them, bus services continue to run between the airport and this London terminal — but checking-in has to be done at the airport.

At Heathrow and many other airports about the world, the new demands of airport security have made their impression upon the rooftop spectators' galleries, and at some international airports these important places are now sadly closed altogether, to be re-opened, perhaps, at happier, unspecified dates in the future. Such places are important to air transport, for apart from providing a point from which a departing relative or friend's aircraft can be watched, the galleries represent the freedom implicit in air transport. Moreover, the airport is usually partly paid for by the taxpayer, who should not be denied the small, sometimes emotional, pleasure of watching an aircraft departure.

Among the numerous facilities for travellers at the airports of the world are car parks — computer-controlled in some places, such as Charles de Gaulle Airport, Paris, while scant in number at others — churches and chapels, which contribute nothing towards airport revenues but much towards some travellers' spiritual tranquility, and intra-airport transit systems, such as those in use at Seattle-Tacoma and Dallas-Fort Worth Airports, which carry passengers between terminals and other parts of the airport on continually running train systems.

Many of the basic services can be improved, such as baggage delivery and flight information, but new ideas such as Airtrans are coming into airports, and a lot more are promised.

Left: Visual flight information boards are an important requirement at international airports, where, because of extraneous noise, audio passenger information system are often almost valueless.

Below left: The withdrawal of baggage check-in facilities at London's West London Air Terminal was a retrograde step in passenger service for travellers, which has only increased the congestion at Heathrow Airport, producing familiar scenes like this.

Below: Baggage delivery at some airports is still practised manually to a Customs hall. Ingenious systems such as this, at Dusseldorf Airport, make baggage recovery quick and trouble-free for the passenger. The carousel or racetrack type baggage-delivery system has been a welcome innovation. Unfortunately, baggage still has to be manhandled to the terminal, and this is where delays usually occur.

Work on the Ground

The parties to ground activities at international airports are primarily the operators, that is the airlines, the airport management organisation itself, and numerous sub-contracting organisations which work for either of these parties. In the case of the airlines, the carriers are concerned with a range of tasks apart from the actual flying of the aeroplanes, ranging from shepherding the passengers on board to fuelling the aircraft and providing in-flight meals for the travellers, who can usually be said to have keen appetites. For the airlines, such services cover check-in and baggage handling, directing and guiding passengers through procedures required by the airport, monitoring the movements of groups (including charter parties), and co-ordinating the movement of these passengers with the ground handling of the aircraft for its task of transporting the passengers away to some other airport.

The majority of airlines perform their own passenger handling services at their national airports, and in some cases at overseas airports as well, but in some instances ground handling agencies perform this task for the carriers. In the UK one such ground handling agency is Servisair, while another is Gatwick Handling. In the Middle East the agency at Dubai Airport is the Dubai National Air Travel Agency, while at Bahrain the local passenger handling company is Bahrain Air Services. The existence of such companies has come about simply because the business of passenger handling has

often become too big a task for individual airlines to cope with.

In scope and sheer volume it would be difficult to calculate the ratio of work done on the ground to that in the air, but an airline's fleet of surface vehicles will often far outnumber the number of aircraft in the carrier's fleet. The vehicles and equipments required for the surface tasks are multifarious. They include baggage conveyors, passenger buses, catering trucks, step units, air starters, crew vans, tractors or airtugs, forklifts, baggage dollies, toilet carts and ground power units. If an airline is essentially a cargo carrier its equipment fleet is likely to include cargo transporters, dollies, elevators, scissor lifts, container transfer vehicles, ULD transporters, mobile conveyors, trailers and forklifts.

Below: The airtug has replaced the apron tractor as the medium for moving very heavy aircraft at airports. These machines may push or pull, and can usually be driven from either end.

Right: An expensive medium for transporting passengers from the airport terminal to the aircraft, albeit an effective one, is the mobile lounge, favoured by some authorities. This model is the Plane-Mate, as used at Baltimore-Washington Airport.

Below right: Most baggage loading has to be performed manually into the aircraft holds. Only with larger aircraft can this airport task be accomplished through containerised methods, thus reducing the possibility of the luggage being damaged.

Many of these vehicles or equipments may be owned by companies which serve the airlines, and a recent trend has seen the establishment of a number of organisations whose purpose in life has been to make available such equipments to airlines on a lease basis at airports in various parts of the world. One of the reasons for this is that the capital cost of the equipments concerned has become too great for some airlines to purchase outright and in any quantity. For major airlines with sometimes as many as 80 outstations, however, there is little choice but to invest in their own substantial fleet of ground vehicles.

For the airport authorities the work on the ground is similarly as heavy in volume as that which it is controlling in the air, and airport authorities the world over equally have sizeable fleets of ground vehicles. These will range from motorised runway sweepers to passenger step units and airbridges, fire-fighting vehicles, administrative cars and airport passenger buses. Vehicles such as the 20,000-gallon fuellers usually belong to the oil companies,

Left: *Just one example of the numerous types of ground equipment used by airlines and airport authorities is this elevating platform specially made for reaching aircraft tails for cleaning and other purposes. Swissair has now retired its Coronado aircraft.*

Below: *The igloo is another creation of the air freighting age, and Japan Air Lines bought a fleet of vehicles especially for the handling of these at its airports. The high speed trucks may carry two pallets or igloos. Igloos here await loading on to the DC-8 freighter.*

who, like various other agencies, work for the airports under contract.

The many tasks of moving passengers through an airport are shared between the managing authority and the carriers with a number of other organisations playing their part. Customs and Immigration will, for example, be the responsibility of the national government agency, while likewise, Security will involve the services of the police — and in some countries even the Army. In some countries the task of bird-scaring is an important matter, and special organisations are employed by the airport specifically for this job. In the case of Security this has become a particular problem in the last 10 years, and different bodies have been varyingly made responsible for the matter, ranging from an airport's own police force to the airlines themselves. Terminal security is now generally regarded as the concern of the airport authority, while security on board the aircraft is the concern of the airlines.

The airport authority is responsible for baggage being moved through the airport while individual airlines may load and unload their own aircraft (and sometimes other airlines' too). Information dissemination in the terminals is the province of the airport authority, as is the provision of car parking facilities, restaurants and luggage repositories. Shops, taxi and car hire services, airport hotels, banks and the actual operation of the restaurants will all be the responsibility of commercial undertakings who work within the airport for the end point of serving the passenger.

At an airport such as Heathrow this can involve more than 50,000 people, which is a measure of the importance of the airport today.

Tranquility in the Air

Every aid or device that is introduced to make flying safer and more efficient brings with it a penalty, in the form of fresh expense to the user and a further complication of the system. Thus, over the past 20 years we have seen in air transport the mandatory introduction of airborne flight recorders, anti-collision lights, triplicated hazard warning and remedial systems, high-definition radars and ground proximity warning systems. It can be said that air transport is the better for the employment of all of these devices, but they have brought a new measure of sophistication to a system in which technology is now said to be running ahead of practical use of the hardware.

Where operational aids are concerned, the airport is now the operator of a multitude of devices, ranging from terminal and airfield surface movement radars to selective calling systems and transmitters to Category IIIa ILS. Even before an airliner is ready for flight it will be under aerodrome control. When the passengers have boarded and the pilot signified readiness for flight, it will be the air traffic controllers at the airport who give him permission for movement away from the terminal and clearance for take-off. He will be directed by the airport to a specified flight level and monitored by airport radar while he is in the terminal area, and until he is handed over to en route air traffic control. At this point the originating airport's responsibilities end.

As he approaches the destination airport he will be observed on control centre radar, brought under the responsibility of approach control for landing, and closely monitored, both visually and audibly,

until ground control indicate that the aircraft is at pierside and the flight ended.

The multitude of devices employed by the airport on the ground to facilitate the passage of 400 ton aircraft carrying upwards of 450 passengers is likewise vast, and includes airfield surface movement radars, runway visual range measurers (RVR), taxiway and runway lighting systems, and their complementary aids, the visual approach slope indicators (VASI). Coupled with these are the instrument landing systems which, brought to a high degree of perfection with Autoland, enable aircraft to take-off and land in zero-visibility conditions. The latest follow-on to this last equipment is the microwave landing system (MLS) and which overcomes the clutter and interference experienced with the more basic ILS and which will permit multi-path approaches. The American-devised Time Reference Scanning Beam system of MLS was selected by ICAO in mid-1978 as the best type to

Below: The air traffic control centre at Brussels, heart of the Eurocontrol system, where lady controllers are employed on traffic monitoring.

Right: Radar coverage of the Dubai region is effected by International Aeradio staff in the control centre at Dubai International Airport. Apart from providing the staff, IAL designed and manufactured the control console.

Below right: A watch over apron movements is maintained from the eyrie in Heathrow's 120ft high control tower. Note runway schematic.

replace existing ILS systems in the 1980s and will now be manufactured for international installation.

The world of air transport has many imperfections, and unfortunately there are still many international airports whose equipment is below the best standards. An airliner taking off from an airport equipped with the very best aids, such as at Heathrow, may well find, therefore, that it is bound for some airport whose basic instrument landing system has not progressed beyond Category II, while its runway lighting system is far from comprehensive. Cost is a factor here, for airport authorities in some countries may have budgets which are slim by comparison with those of wealthier air-faring nations.

In this regard the United Nations agency, ICAO, performs a valuable task through its airport development programmes, which have enabled many airports to be brought up to standards which they might otherwise not have met for the supersonic age. IATA, too, has made its contribution to the development of less well-equipped airports, both in their planning and management.

For the future, more aids and devices will be required and will be installed at the world's airports to meet the needs of a business which is daily seeing more airliners in the air and calling for high-speed reactions on the part of pilots. With supersonic airliners amongst these aircraft the margin for error is narrowing.

In spite of the fact that the world civil aviation fleet has gone up from under 3,000 aircraft in 1946 to over 9,000 in 1978, air transport is, nevertheless, becoming safer in statistical terms every day, and in terms of passenger fatalities per 100 million passenger-kilometres was down to 0.08 in 1977. Another way of illustrating this improvement is to record that 821 people were killed world-wide on scheduled passenger flights in 1976 compared with 845 in the year 1960. The big difference here is that 580 million passengers were carried on scheduled flights in 1976 compared with 100 million in 1960.

From its humble beginnings, just 60 years ago, air transport has become not only a highly attractive medium of travel but a safe one, and it is not surprising therefore that the world's airports have blossomed into the remarkable places that they are today, as the following pages illustrate.

Right: Plessey AR-15 S-band medium range surveillance radar.

Below: Thomson-CSF equipment is installed in Copenhagen's air traffic control centre. Radar scopes now provide labelled aircraft information.

Right: *Dallas-Fort Worth Airport, which is built, literally, between the two American cities. The two, main, parallel runways are bisected by a spine road, called the International Parkway.*

Below: *Just one of the thousands of tasks performed 24 hours a day by airport staff, the positioning of aircraft. This is alternatively effected by an apron control officer located in a terminal tower and in radio contact with the aircraft's pilot.*

Part Two

Statistics

Major Airports of the World: Ranking by Traffic Volume, 1977

Ranking	Airport	Number of Passengers in 000s
1	Chicago O'Hare	44,238
2	Atlanta International	29,977
3	Los Angeles	28,361
4	London Heathrow	23,775
5	Tokyo Haneda	23,190
6	New York JFK	22,545
7	San Francisco International	20,249
8	Dallas/Fort Worth	17,318
9	Denver	15,281
10	New York La Guardia	15,087
11	Frankfurt	14,976
12	Osaka	13,935
13	Miami	13,736
14	Washington National	12,612
15	Paris Orly	12,557
16	Toronto	12,305
17	Honolulu	12,208
18	Boston	12,191
19	Rome Fiumicino	10,473
20	Madrid	9,373

Major Airports of the World: Ranking by Aircraft Movements, 1977

Ranking	Airport	Number
1	Chicago O'Hare	749,278
2	Atlanta International	476,237
3	Los Angeles	431,811
4	Dallas/Fort Worth	320,000
5	Denver	302,400
6	New York JFK	294,100
7	San Francisco International	290,800
8	Boston	250,200
9	Philadelphia	244,368
10	London Heathrow	243,000
11	New York La Guardia	238,900
12	Miami	234,000
13	St Louis	222,222
14	Washington National	212,000
15	Frankfurt	201,765
16	Toronto	175,700
17	Detroit	166,600
18	Paris Orly	161,900
19	Kansas City	149,700
20	Rome Fiumicino	142,095

Major Airports of the World: Ranking by Cargo Handled, 1977

Ranking	Airport	Annual Tonnage Handled
1	New York JFK	1,191,035
2	Los Angeles	812,283
3	Chicago O'Hare	702,999
4	Frankfurt	541,000
5	Miami	448,000
6	Tokyo Haneda	443,400
7	London Heathrow	442,100
8	Montreal Dorval	420,000
9	San Francisco International	392,000
10	Atlanta	326,000

Traffic at United Kingdom Airports, 1977

Airport	Number of passengers handled in 000s	Cargo tonnage handled
Aberdeen	948	5,900
Belfast	1,039	14,000
Birmingham	1,065	3,200
Bristol	223	2,400
East Midlands	684	8,000
Edinburgh	1,021	1,300
Gatwick	6,652	100,405
Glasgow	1,752	17,000
Guernsey, CI	500	9,400
Isle of Man	353	2,600
Jersey, CI	1,420	11,314
Leeds/Bradford	282	400
Liverpool	273	11,900
London Heathrow	23,775	442,100
Luton	1,951	3,300
Manchester	2,903	37,468
Newcastle	741	4,700
Prestwick	386	17,300
Southend	240	6,400
Stansted	299	27,600
Tees-side	218	500

Part Three

Abu Dhabi International

UAE

Location: 7.5 miles SE of Abu Dhabi
Elevation: 13ft (4m)
Runways in use: 1
13/31 10,496ft × 150ft (3,200m × 45m)
Passengers handled in 1977: 837,059
Total aircraft movements in 1975: 43,000
Cargo handled in 1977: 25,253 tons

Of the seven states forming the United Arab Emirates, the biggest and the official capital is Abu Dhabi. A new airport is being built there according to plans prepared by the consultancy division of the Paris Airport Authority to handle up to three million passengers a year, but until this airport is opened (about 1981), the existing airport is being enlarged and improved.

This was opened in August 1970 and, like some of its Middle Eastern contemporaries, is a beautiful creation, built by a British construction company. The present terminal is currently handling a total of over 800,000 passengers a year. The terminal complex consists of three floors, accommodating departure and arrival lounges on a single level, with government and airline offices above. A VIP lounge and restaurant is on a third level. The control tower with air traffic services, meteorology and communications are housed in a structure incorporated into the terminal complex. Separately, there is a cargo building, a maintenance and overhaul building and a fire station, together with a large steel hangar. The whole airport is managed by the British firm of International Aeradio Limited under a contract with the Emirate of Abu Dhabi. The air traffic control services are performed by this well-known British company which also manufactured most of the ATC consoles in use in the tower. For long under British protection, the Gulf States now have an excellent commercial and operational association with British companies such as IAL, who also provide training in airport management skills for Gulf airport personnel.

Until the new airport is brought into service, the terminal at Abu Dhabi Airport is being extended to handle the growing traffic passing through Abu Dhabi, carried principally by the TriStars of national carrier Gulf Air and British Airways. Traffic supervision and cargo handling is performed by Gulf Air, with whom the Abu Dhabi Government has a contract for this purpose.

Below: Abu Dhabi International was opened in 1970, but such is traffic growth that a new airport is under construction, for opening about 1981.

Amsterdam (Schiphol)

Netherlands

Location: 6 miles SW of Amsterdam
Elevation: 13ft (4m) *below* sea level
Runways in use: 4
09/27 11,325ft × 200ft (3,453m × 60m)
06/24 10,824ft × 200ft (3,244m × 60m)
01L/19R 10,640ft × 200ft (3,300m × 60m)
01R/19L, 11,150ft × 200ft (3,400m × 60m)
Airport area: 4,325 acres
Passengers handled in 1977: 8,931,985
Total aircraft movements in 1977: 136,329
Cargo handled in 1977: 274,396 tons

There has been talk for some time in the Netherlands about the idea of creating a second major airport for Holland, but the Schiphol Airport Authority has no doubts that the principal airport now operating can cope with all traffic currently projected for up to, and probably beyond, the year 2000. If this proves so, Schiphol Airport will have been serving international air transport for the best part of 100 years.

Amsterdam's international airport lies on what was once the Haarlem Lake, which 400 years ago was a battle area for ships of the Prince of Orange and the Spanish fleet. The Haarlem Lake was drained in 1852, and the largest land reclamation operation then performed in the Netherlands was carried out. The task took five years. A stronghold was erected in the north-east corner and given the old name of Schiphol, which literally meant 'ships hole', or the grave of ships. In 1917 a military aerodrome was laid out at the foot of this strongpoint and also took the name Schiphol. Then, three years later, the Dutch airline KLM began services from the airfield, and the site's life as a civil airport had begun.

As KLM developed, the airport became marked as the international airport for Amsterdam, and because it was so favourably located and in an area of completely flat terrain (Schiphol Airport is actually 13ft below sea level) it was ideal for its purpose.

Schiphol's site was also ideal for future development, and this development has been taking place progressively since 1926. In 1938 Schiphol became the second airport after Bromma (Stockholm) to have a system of paved, hard surfaced runways, and that year its original 190 acres were expanded to 520 acres. Today, the airport covers 4,325 acres, and is a Dutch showcase for international air traffic. In 1967 a completely new terminal complex was opened on what is now called Schiphol Centrum, and to the north-west of the previous facilities. Apart from providing a completely modernised terminal area for airport users, and which area offered a massive cargo warehouse,

Below: One of the most important airports in Europe, Schiphol, Amsterdam, has been serving air transport since the beginning of commercial aviation in 1920. The Airport Authority building is on the left; Schipol Hilton to the right, and flanked by Aviodome, the airport's National Aviation Museum.

Previous page: *Schiphol's original Pier B's Y-shaped end has been matched by a similar addition to Piers A (lower left) and D (top right) and Pier C will be modified in the future. Circular building is station terminal to provide a direct Amsterdam rail link by 1979.*

Above: *Cargo handling at Schiphol.*

administration block, hotels and airline blocks, the developed central area also gave full scope to the tangential runway scheme, which provided for four runways disposed around the terminal facilities.

With the new terminal scheme, three piers were built, with a north and south pier on either side of a central pier, Pier B. The central pier was bifurcated at its extremity. All three piers had initial provision for 25 aircraft parking places. The first straight section of the central pier was equipped with a moving walkway for passengers. Holding lounges for departing passengers were arranged in the piers near each aircraft position.

In 1971, in order to provide for the wide-bodied jets and the traffic they were bringing, the southerly pier, Pier A, was extended with a short 'head' at its extremity, bifurcated in similar manner to the central pier. This added nine aircraft parking positions to raise the capacity of the terminal complex to approximately eight million passengers a year.

In order to provide further capacity, the terminal buildings were enlarged by 120% and as a feature of this extra work a completely new pier, Pier D, was constructed to the north, especially for wide-bodied aircraft, and further raising the capacity of the airport to 18 million passengers a year. The number of aircraft parking positions at the four piers A, B, C, and D was increased to 42. These extensions were introduced into service in April 1975, at which date 56 airlines were using the airport.

In 1974 work on the construction of a railway connection between Schiphol and the city of Amsterdam was begun and was scheduled to be completed in 1978. This rail link is to be joined about 1981 by a connection between the airport and The Hague. These rail services will provide additional services for the passenger to the airport buses, operated by KLM and which connect with Amsterdam railway station.

Schiphol Airport is now one of the busiest airports in Europe handling almost nine million passengers a year, and is one of the most attractive. It also has many interesting features, not the least of which is its history and location, and which include the airport's own national aviation museum, and probably the biggest (and possibly also the cheapest) duty-free shopping centre in Europe. The airport is also third busiest in Europe in terms of annual freight tonnage handled.

Ankara (Esenboga)   Turkey

Location: 17 miles NE of Ankara
Elevation: 3,108ft (949m)
Runways in use: 1
03/21 12,306ft × 200ft (3,752m × 60m)
Passengers handled in 1977: 1,427,278
Total aircraft movements in 1977: 23,074
Cargo handled in 1977: 17,126 tons

Domestic traffic forms the bulk of the traffic handled at Ankara's Esenboga, one explanation for which is that much of this is carried on by government officials. In 1977 the actual figures were 1,069,964 domestic passengers and 357,314 international travellers. In terms of movements, Ankara Airport similarly handles about half the number at Istanbul. The airport for Ankara was opened in 1955 and is typical of the design of this period, with a long terminal building having a principal entry and departure gate, and incorporating a central structure surmounted by the airport control tower. The airport works well enough, however, and is open 24 hours a day. It is located 17 miles from the city of Ankara, has one runway, and an apron capacity for nine B707-types at one time.

Both Istanbul and Ankara see a fair amount of military aircraft movements as well as civil, and at Ankara these are amounting to some 1,500 military arrivals and departures annually.

Below: Ankara's Esenboga Airport handles more domestic passengers than international.

Athens (Hellenikon/Spata)   Greece

HELLENIKON
Location: 8 miles from Athens city centre
Elevation: 89ft (27m)
Runways in use: 2
15/33 11,550ft × 200ft (3,520m × 60m)
03/21 5,940ft × 200ft (1,810m × 60m)
Passengers handled in 1977: 7,120,000 (estimated)
Total aircraft movements in 1977: 99,000
Cargo handled in 1977: 53,000 tons

SPATA
Location: 17 miles from Athens city centre
Runways: 2
13,120ft × 150ft (4,000m × 45m) parallel
Airport to be opened for traffic in 1985

The sun has always figured prominently in Greek aviation, from the time of the legend of Daedalus and Icarus whose elation on flying on wings of feathers and wax led them to disaster. Icarus came to know the power of the sun, and several million tourists have felt its attraction over the years as they have flown into Greece's principal airport on pleasure bent.

The present airport at Hellenikon was built on the coast, just eight miles from the centre of Athens, in 1936, when the modest facilities erected then comprised a single runway, a few hundred feet in length, and two small terminals.

Immediately after the war, in 1945, development work on new and better premises began, but a halt was called to further work in 1950 with the decision to review the future potential of the site. A feasibility study for further expansion was approved in 1958 as the new big jet aircraft were coming on the scene, and a new construction programme was put in hand with the decision to retain the present airport site. It was decided also to purchase extensive additional areas of land to the east and south, and in 1962, with financial and technical assistance from the US Government, further development was made. The complete eastern sector of land was taken up for the construction of a new international terminal, while the original buildings on the north-west were retained for exclusive use by national carrier Olympic Airways.

This is the arrangement to the present day, with the international terminal — designed by famous Finnish architect Saarinen — seeing an increasing number of international arrivals annually. This terminal, which was inaugurated in 1969, had become so busy by 1975 that enlargement was considered necessary. At that date it was handling 1,201,000 tourists alone every year. In 1976 Hellenikon handled well over six million passengers of all categories, this traffic representing 70% of the total air passenger traffic through Greece.

This growth in air traffic has made its mark, however, and by the beginning of the 1970s it was clear that Hellenikon's days were numbered if traffic was to go on increasing at the present rate. The urgency for a new airport was eased with the introduction of the first wide-bodied jets and then the cut-back in flights at the time of the fuel crisis, but the lovely country of Greece is a strong attraction for tourists, and when air transport recovered its earlier buoyancy the pressure was on Athens' airport once again.

Passenger traffic at Athens has been growing at an average annual rate of 11% for the past 10 years, and because of the resulting congestion it was understood that the improvements made could be nothing more than stop-gap actions until the day when a new airport was built to take over. Hellenikon has two runways with a bearing strength of 45,000kg SIWL, or enough to take the heaviest jets, and expansion of the apron has made it sufficient to handle six Boeing 747s at once.

Apart from its limitations in size, however, Hellenikon presented problems by its airport noise, and in the past few years this has become a major issue. Because of the pressure over noise pollution and a recognition of the nuisance this causes to residents of resort areas such as Glyfada and Vouliagmeni, the Greek Government rejected proposals to further extend the life of Hellenikon, and finally pronounced that it must close. This is expected by 1985, and the Government has said that the old airport will then be demolished, in 1990.

A master plan for a new airport was drawn up by three parties, under contract to the Hellenic Civil Aviation Authority, namely the Aéroport de Paris, Flughafen Frankfurt AG, and a Greek planning concern ADK. With final approval for this plan the new airport will be built on a site at Spata, approximately 17 miles from the city of Athens. The whole project is expected to cost some three billion Drachma.

Four sites were studied for a replacement for Hellenikon, at Tanagra, Vari, Spata and Lavrion, and for a variety of reasons three were rejected in favour of Spata, even though that site is almost twice the distance from Athens compared to Hellenikon. If the Spata Airport is built according to the present plan, a motorway will be built also, to give high-speed connection. The new airport will be two and a half times the size of Hellenikon and handle traffic up to the year 2000. The airport will have two 13,000ft long parallel runways, with 5,000ft separation between them, and simultaneous take-offs and landings will be practised as traffic dictates. The initial handling capability of Spata will be for 15 million passengers a year.

There will be three circular terminal areas at Spata, with four holding lounges spaced around the apron and stretching from these terminals. The terminal areas will be spaced in a straight line and flanked by the parallel runways. On the other side of the access road from Athens and leading to the terminal areas there will be a maintenance area, adjoined by workshops and parking ramps, and at this end of one runway there will be a cargo terminal and a general aviation facility. At the extreme end of the airport will be the fuel farm. Spata airport is expected to be open by 1985.

Below: *The aircraft parking area at Athens Airport, which is the operational headquarters of the national carrier, Olympic Airways. Olympic operates some 22 aircraft, in a mixed fleet of B707s, B727s, B747s and YS-11s.*

Auckland International (Mangere)   New Zealand

Location: 13.5 miles south of Auckland
Elevation: 23ft (7m)
Runways in use: 1
05/23 10,800ft x 150ft (3,295m x 45m)
Airport area: 1,300 acres
Passengers handled in 1977: 1,784,811
Total aircraft movements in 1977: 76,066
Cargo handled in 1977: 49,356 tons

As the largest city in New Zealand, Auckland might be expected to boast an imposing international airport, and in fact the traffic passing through Mangere has made this the busiest international airport in the country. The city's size aside, contributing factors towards the busyness of Auckland International include the activity of Air New Zealand, the country's flag carrier, which has both its head office and operational headquarters in Auckland. Thus, this is the originating and terminating point for ANZ's international flights.

In terms of air transport history Auckland International is a young airport, for work on the site was only begun in 1960 and the airport was opened for business in its first stage of development in November 1965. The actual official opening date was 29 January 1966. Prior to this civil air services had taken place from the original RNZAF airfield at Whenuapai, which became unsuitable for air transport operations on a large scale.

The preliminary construction work took almost three years, and this included the reclamation of 160 acres of Manukaua Harbour, into which part of the airport was built to avoid absorbing more farmland than necessary. In this reclamation task 6.2 million cubic yards of rock and volcanic scoria were transferred from an extinct volcano on nearby Pukitutu Island.

In the first two weeks after the official opening, 10,000 passengers passed through Mangere Airport on 145 international flights, which served as an augury of the activity in store for New Zealand's principal international airport, and this promise has been fulfilled over the years since. By 1970 passenger traffic had reached over one million a year, and this was up to 1.3 million by 1972. In 1978 traffic was totalling almost two million passengers annually, with 76,000 movements a year, a far cry from the 250,000 passengers recorded in the first year of operation.

Development has been phased at Mangere, with 24 buildings constructed in the first years of service, among them Air New Zealand's engineering hangar, which was the largest structure at the airport. The first passenger terminal was constructed from the outset as a temporary facility, with an intended life in the passenger-handling role of some five years. The purpose-built passenger terminal is now in service, and this unlovely building features an associate pier structure stretching across the apron and serving passenger aircraft by way of airbridges. This terminal is located to the west of the earlier terminal, which has now become a cargo terminal.

Other buildings erected as part of the complete Auckland airport development scheme include the operations building, radio receiving and transmitting stations, meteorological building, fire station, catering building and electrical sub-stations. There is an adjoining fuel farm, airline office buildings and an adequate collection of car parks. The tallest structure at the airport is the 104ft control tower, which has a control room 86ft up.

A feature of the site at Mangere, from which the airport takes its local name, is nearby Mount Mangere, which resembles a reclining man. The word *Mangere* is Maori for 'lazy', and the spot is said to have been named after this languorous image.

Below: *Less than beautiful to the eye, but functional for all that, is Auckland International's airport terminal building, which is one of the most recent structures at New Zealand's developing, principal international airport.*

Bahrain International (Muharraq)

Bahrain

Location: 3.5 miles from Manama city
Elevation: 5ft (1.5m)
Runways in use: 1
12/30 12,520ft × 200ft (3,816m × 60m)
Passengers handled in 1977: 1,880,000
Total aircraft movements in 1977: 35,400
Cargo handled in 1977: 27,170 tons

Bahrain earned a new place in the air transport history books when on 21 January 1976 it became the terminating point for British Airways' first supersonic Concorde service from London. When Britain and France began Concorde services on that historic day, in easterly and westerly directions, British Airways chose Bahrain as a stopping place on the long route to Singapore and Australia — the airline's ultimate objective.

The island State of Bahrain has, however, been a very important place in air transport for almost 40 years, for, in the days when Imperial Airways was forging air links to India and beyond, Bahrain was chosen by British Airways' original predecessor as the most suitable location in the Gulf for a major transit base, firstly for landplane and then flying-boat operations. From that time until just a decade ago, Britain's military presence was also strong, and the RAF force at Muharraq substantial.

Much of the former RAF camp is still used at the aerodrome, but today for civil aviation purposes, housing airline and administrative agency offices, which are all joined by an imposing international airport terminal.

It is through this terminal that pass the very many airline passengers travelling to and from Bahrain in an increasing tide, as the country's commercial importance grows, and which now make Bahrain International one of the newly important airports in the world. As a Gulf State in its own right, Bahrain's prosperity is based on oil, which was first discovered in the country in 1932. Since the fuel crisis of 1973-74, however, this liquid gold has assumed new importance and the country's development bears witness to the prosperity the new demand is bringing.

The development of Bahrain International has gone hand-in-hand with this new interest, for in the last few years both passenger and cargo traffic have soared. This surge of traffic required an urgent expansion of the airport terminal, apron and operational facilities, and while much work has been done in this direction even more is required, and is being put in hand. When Concorde services began this increased the airport's importance further, and large sums of money were allocated by the Bahrain Government.

In terms of traffic, Bahrain's passenger throughput rocketed, from 274,526 passengers in 1972 to 1,650, 000 in 1976. In 1977, it had gone up further to 1,880,000. Similarly, cargo traffic has soared, from the 5,000 tons handled in 1972 to the 27,000 tons moved through the airport in 1977. There was no less than a 52% increase in cargo tonnage handled in 1977 over 1976.

Because of this new movement, the British-built terminal building was given a new wing in 1976, and it was also provided with passenger loading bridges, to enable terminal-to-aircraft passenger loading to supersede the old procedure of passengers simply walking across the apron and up steps.

The terminal building now is expansive, airy and well-equipped with waiting facilities, restaurants and duty-free stores for passengers in their passage from the city to other places. Passenger flow requires departing travellers to pass through ticketing procedures on the ground floor, and thence up stairs to the departure lounge, from which exit is made by way of an airbridge to the cabin of the aircraft on the ramp. Outgoing baggage is processed through the building at ground level. Incoming passengers leave the aircraft cabin by the airbridges, and proceed from the arrivals hall of the building down stairs for baggage recovery. On the landside they take a taxi to the city. There is no airline bus service.

Some 23 international airlines operate to Bahrain, and to improve further the facilities at the airport both the Bahraini Government and a new agency, Bahrain Airport Services, have embarked upon a major investment programme, involving six million Bahraini Dinars (approximately £7.9 million). This money will be spent on a purpose-built cargo terminal, an aircraft maintenance building, a new fuel farm, and a new inventory of ground support equipment. The ground handling equipment will be bought steadily by the Bahrain Airport Services company, which was formed in July 1977 and granted the rights for all ground handling and ramp services at the airport by the Bahrain Government. The company took over this function from ASGUL (Airport Services Gulf), a subsidiary company of Gulf Air, which airline has its headquarters at Bahrain. BAS is a private company, with no government involvement, and which apart from performing ramp handling, operates the cargo warehouse, the airport restaurant and the flight kitchen — which produces no fewer than 12,000 airline meals a day. In taking over the work of ASGUL, BAS inherited a collection of various items of ground equipment, and plans to rationalise and modernise this equipment holding gradually. It is interesting to know that Concorde required no special equipment at all when it began its services, which in 1978 were at a frequency of three a week from London.

Above right: Bahrain Airport terminal building, from the landside.

Right: British Airways' Concorde services were partly instrumental in promoting further development of Bahrain International, already one of the busiest airports in the Gulf area.

Baltimore-Washington International USA

Location: 10 miles south of Baltimore, 30 miles north of Washington DC
Elevation: 144ft (44m)
Runways in use: 4
10/28 9,450ft × 200ft (2,880m × 60m)
15R/33L 9,500ft × 150ft (2,895m × 45m)
4/22 6,000ft × 150ft (1,828m × 45m)
15L/33R 3,010ft × 75ft (917m × 23m) (general aviation)
Airport area: 3,200 acres
Passengers handled in 1977: 3,238,994
Total aircraft movements in 1977: 240,658
Cargo handled in 1977: 65,365 tons

Aviation began in Baltimore, Maryland, as long ago as 1784, when according to the records of the Maryland State Aviation Administration, a 13-year-old boy named Edward Warren lifted into the air on 24 June of that year in a balloon owned by a local attorney. The historic event is said to have occurred at Mount Vernon Place, about 12 miles north of where Baltimore-Washington Airport stands today.

The first airport for Baltimore was actually opened in September 1921. A municipal airport for the city was planned, but because of the Depression this did not actually open until 1941, by which time aircraft were already bigger and faster, and an even better airport was thus thought desirable. A master plan for this airport was submitted in May 1946 and construction of this began on a 3,200-acre site 10 miles south of Baltimore and 30 miles north of Washington DC. This airport was opened on 24 June 1950 by President Harry S. Truman and was officially named Friendship International Airport.

Below: *Once called Friendship Airport, Baltimore's airport is now known as Baltimore-Washington International. This aerial view shows the new terminal construction.*

Since that time, Friendship International has become famous in American air transport circles because of the facilities provided to meet the first demands of the jet age, and which enabled record-breaking flights to be made by the first Boeing 707s. Situated in the centre of an area with a population of more than five million, Friendship International was the only jet airport for the Baltimore-Washington region until 1962. By the early 1970s it was clear that the finance for extensive capital improvements being required should be provided by the State of Maryland, and on 26 July 1972, therefore, the State of Maryland purchased the airport from the city of Baltimore for $36 million.

Following this the role of the airport was reappraised, and it was decided that a prime objective was to develop the airport for the future to serve effectively the residents of all areas of Maryland as well as the Federal Capitol of Washington and surrounding states. To reflect this role the airport was renamed Baltimore-Washington International on 16 November 1973. At the same time a far-reaching expansion and modernisation programme for the airport's passenger terminal was put in hand, at a cost of approximately $65 million.

Under the plan the new terminal will be 75% larger than the earlier facility. The architectural concept for the structure's exterior revolves around glass and steel, to give an airy and spacious feeling and admit plenty of light, the planners' intention being to eliminate the sight of any buff-coloured brick in the structure.

The expanded passenger terminal will be capable of handling over 11 million passengers annually.

Construction work began in October 1974 and was scheduled to be completed by 1979. The glass walls will allow approaching passengers to identify readily the location of airline ticket counters, and 10 new entrances will give direct access to these new airline ticket counter locations, which will be so positioned as to decrease passenger walking distances by 60%. Aircraft gate positions will be increased in number, and all gates equipped with passenger holding lounges. In addition, each airline using the airport will have its own separate baggage claim location on the lower level of the terminal, a feature which would undoubtedly be welcomed at other airports as a means of dramatically reducing the time spent by passengers waiting for baggage, time which in many areas of the world is becoming intolerable.

The new international arrivals wing will incorporate passenger holding rooms for international and charter flights as well as a tax-free shop. There will be enlarged Customs, public health and immigration facilities. Aircraft gate positions will be increased to 27 in number and boarding gates will be equipped with passenger loading bridges. In addition, two mobile lounges, will be used to carry travellers to their parked aircraft.

Other work that has been taking place at Baltimore-Washington includes the construction of a $5 million air cargo complex with 110,000sq ft of covered floor space, which was completed in July 1974, expansion of the car parks to provide for 3,500 cars, and a $4.5 million runway and taxiway improvement scheme, carried out in the autumn of 1973, and which included installation of Category II ILS facilities.

Brussels National (Zaventem)   Belgium

Location: 7.5 miles NE of Brussels
Elevation: 80ft (55m)
Runways in use: 4
02/20 9,247ft × 165ft (2,819m × 50m)
08R/26L 10,530ft × 150ft (3,211m × 45m)
08L/26R 11,930ft × 150ft (3,638m × 45m)
12/30 8,213ft × 150ft (2,504m × 45m)
Airport area: 2,717 acres
Passengers handled in 1977: 4,449,000
Total aircraft movements in 1977: 104,700
Cargo handled in 1977: 128,000 tons

The capital city of Belgium has become of greater importance to European nations in recent years as the administrative heart of the European Economic Community, and much of the new air traffic generated by EEC comings and goings has benefited Brussels National.

The airport is the international air gateway for Belgium and was developed from the former military airfield of Zaventem in 1945. By 1956 the growth of air traffic called for a fresh development scheme, and a fine new terminal was planned. This new terminal, which incorporated the airport control tower, opened in 1961 but was largely destroyed by fire in early 1962. A reconstruction job was put in hand, however, and passenger handling was carried on in temporary facilities until the building was freshly opened.

The airport today is an attractive one for the traveller, offering comfortable passenger halls and waiting areas and with the desirable features of good restaurants and an excellent duty free shop. In 1973 the main terminal was augmented by a satellite terminal remoted somewhat from the main building and reached by a passenger pier, which is equipped with moving walkways. This radial terminal serves the aircraft which park around it by the medium of telescopic airbridges.

Further terminal developments are planned for Brussels National, although airport development is constrained somewhat by land limitations. One passenger facility worth mentioning is the hotel located within the transit hall of the airport building. Brussels airport is thus among those relatively few world airports which have their own airport hotel, situated on the airport site.

A particularly important area of traffic at Brussels in the last few years has been that of cargo, and the Belgium Airports and Airways Agency, which operates Brussels National Airport, erected a large cargo warehouse in 1965, with a capacity of 120,000 tons/year. Cargo traffic at Brussels National reached 115,000 tons in 1970, whereafter expansion of the cargo warehouse and cargo handling facilities was undertaken. The national airline SABENA, which handles the largest proportion of air cargo passing through the airport, also introduced its own cargo handling facilities, and the overall effort is now providing for the movement of 128,000 tons of air cargo a year. In 1976 the dramatic growth of air cargo at Brussels was evident from the 27% increase over 1975; this was the second largest growth among European airports for the year, next to Dusseldorf.

Below: *The comfortable hall of the main departure lounge at Brussels National Airport, gateway airport to the heart of the European Economic Community.*

Chicago International (O'Hare)   USA

Location: 15 miles NW of Chicago
Elevation: 667ft (203m)
Runways in use: 7
14R/32L 11,600ft x 200ft (3,536m x 60m)
14L/32R 10,000ft x 150ft (3,048m x 45m)
9R/27L 10,140ft x 150ft (3,090m x 45m)
9L/27R 7,415ft x 150ft (2,260m x 45m)
4R/22L 8,070ft x 150ft (2,460m x 45m)
4L/22R 8,500ft x 150ft (2,590 x 45m)
18 (STOL) 5,341 x 150ft (1,628m x 45m)
Airport area: 7,000 acres
Passengers handled in 1977: 44,238,019
Total aircraft movements in 1977: 749,278
Cargo handled in 1977: 702,999 tons

Over the years, Chicago O'Hare has retained its place as the busiest airport in the world, and continues to leave other airports standing in terms of both the number of passengers handled and air transport movements annually. As figures show, O'Hare is a very busy cargo airport also, and second only to New York's John F. Kennedy Airport in tonnage handled amongst major airports. The sheer volume of activity is almost unbelievable in its immensity. In 1977 over 44 million passengers were handled on domestic, international, commuter and other air carrier flights in a total of 749,278 aircraft movements. In 1977 also 703,000 tons of cargo were moved on domestic and international flights. Every day, 100,000 passengers (together with about the same number of visitors) pass through O'Hare Airport, with the air passengers using the services of 26 major airlines, seven commuter operators, four supplemental carriers and a number of helicopter and other air carrier companies. There is an average of 1,900 aircraft arrivals and departures daily.

All of this development has occurred since the end of World War II, when Chicago City Council bought land and some facilities from the US Government as war surplus. What is now the site of Chicago's O'Hare Airport was originally known as Orchard Place, and which had been built during World War II by the Douglas Aircraft Company for the production of military transports. When the installation was declared surplus by the War Assets Administration, the city planners recognised that, because of its location and terrain, Orchard Place had the potential for development as a major airport for Chicago and to augment the existing Midway Airport, which was already under pressure. In January 1949, $2.5 million was authorised for new construction work, and the O'Hare Airport story had begun.

O'Hare opened its doors to domestic aviation traffic in October 1955. The name of Lt Commander Edward H. O'Hare, the United States' greatest naval hero, was conferred on the airport in December 1958, at which time international jet flights were

Above: The 7,000-acre spread of Chicago O'Hare International Airport, illustrating well the terminal and pier arrangement and car park lots, which provide for 14,000 cars. The Rotunda building, which houses restaurants and cocktail lounges, is clearly seen between Terminals 2 and 3, which handle domestic traffic. The international Terminal 1, with its accompanying Y-shaped pier, is at the opposing end of the complex. There are seven active runways.

beginning to make their impact, and the future role of O'Hare as an international terminal was recognised.

The first expansion programme at O'Hare was begun in 1959, and by 1961 traffic at the airport had surpassed that at Midway to make O'Hare the busiest airport in the world. In 1963 the present terminal complex was dedicated in the presence of President John F. Kennedy. A new control tower almost 200ft high was built in 1971 and the runway system steadily enlarged from four to the present seven runways. Today, the whole complex of Chicago International covers 7,000 acres, and employs the services of over 33,000 people.

All scheduled passenger activity at O'Hare is concentrated in three main terminal buildings. International flights are handled in Terminal 1 while domestic flights are handled in Terminals 2 and 3. The buildings are linked together on the upper level enabling passage from one terminal to the next; there is also a free shuttle bus service for those who prefer to ride. The commuter airlines serving various midwest destinations operate from an ancillary terminal, as does Butler Aviation which handles general aviation activity at the airport, including private and corporate aircraft operations.

The sheer size of O'Hare makes it an impressive facility, with its Y-shaped pier structures on either side of a main terminal and vast parking lot on the landside capable of accommodating over 14,000 cars, some of them in what is the largest elevated parking structure of its kind in the world. For passengers there are numerous snack bars and cafeterias open 24 hours a day on the upper and lower levels of each terminal building, but in the Rotunda, a circular building located between Terminals 2 and 3, there are several restaurants and cocktail lounges on the upper and mezzanine levels. There is an O'Hare Hilton Hotel located directly opposite the main terminal complex, and this, of course, offers a further variety of restaurant facilities. The O'Hare Hilton has over 900 guest rooms, together with an arcade of shops on its lower level. It is reached by the pedestrian tunnels on the lower level of Terminal 2.

Other airport facilities include an inter-denominational chapel in Terminal 2; first aid stations, which include provision for nursing mothers; lost and found counters; airport information booths employing multi-lingual receptionists; 500 public telephones; US mail boxes in each terminal

and two public observation decks which are open year-round from 8am to 9.30pm daily.

Other facilities at O'Hare include a main fire station with two satellite facilities, operated by the Chicago Fire Department, which allow fire fighters to reach any part of the field within three minutes. There is an air cargo area, comprising 13 separate cargo buildings, which house 27 airlines and six freight forwarders. The US Postal Service maintains its largest airport facility at O'Hare, and which handles 172,000 tons of mail yearly.

The seven runways at the airport include three sets of parallel runways and which range in length from 5,340ft to 11,600ft. The control tower oversees the operation of almost 800,000 aircraft movements each year. There are 27 operating positions in this tower, eight in the tower cab and 19 in the radar room. There are 125 air traffic controllers in the tower and 70 electronics technicians. ATC at the airport is the responsibility of the Federal Aviation Administration.

Chicago International is giving fresh attention to the task of handling future traffic and new consideration is being devoted to a plan for further use of Midway Airport. With the growing amount of traffic at Chicago's airports, an earlier plan provided for a new airport on an island site in Lake Michigan, but it is now felt that better use can be made of the existing airports, which include the third airport at Meigs Field. A new study of Midway's potential indicates it could handle up to 10 million passengers annually, instead of the current 800,000, while Meigs Field might increase further its contribution to Chicago, which in financial terms is now considered to be $44 million annually. Meigs Fields is situated on an island covering 72 acres and located only 15 minutes from Chicago city centre. It handles over 386,000 passengers annually and holds the title of the world's busiest single-runway airport.

The master plan for the long-term use and development of all three airports is scheduled for completion by the end of 1979.

Christchurch International

New Zealand

Location: 6 miles from Christchurch city centre
Elevation: 115ft (35m)
Runways in use: 2
01/20 8,010ft × 150ft (2,442m × 45m) (to be lengthened to 9,840ft, 3,000m)
11/29 5,700ft × 150ft (1,737m × 45m)
Airport area: 1,870 acres
Passengers handled in 1977: 1,190,003
Total aircraft movements in 1977: 28,607
Cargo handled in 1977: 17,159 tons

The city of Christchurch in the South Island of New Zealand took an active interest in aviation from the days prior to World War I, and has had an airport since 1936. Sir Henry Wigram, a former mayor of the city, formed the Canterbury Aviation Company at the time of World War I and trained more than 100 pilots for the Commonwealth war effort. In 1927 the Canterbury Aero Club was formed, the first of its kind in the country, and further impetus was given to New Zealand aviation.

In 1935 the Christchurch City Council decided in principle on establishing an airport, and selected the present site. With considerable foresight, the Council took into account factors which seemed important to the siting of an airport, namely, good proximity to the city, an area which offered room for expansion, ready approaches from the air, and flat terrain free from surrounding hills. In 1936 the first land was acquired for the airport, and a 3,000ft runway laid. A wooden terminal building was erected. Harewood Airport, as the airport was then known, was opened for commercial flying in 1940, and has been steadily expanded and improved ever since.

The airport became a training station for airmen during World War II, and after the war the Christchurch City Council purchased more land and extended the flying areas. In 1950, 100 years after the arrival at the nearby port of Lyttelton of the first four ships with settlers from Britain, the Prime Minister of New Zealand redesignated the airfield an international airport.

In 1954 the need for a new terminal building became paramount and, with the New Zealand Government sharing the cost of this equally with the Christchurch City Council, the new terminal was erected. It was introduced into service fully in 1960, and further additions have been made since; in 1975 extensions were made to the domestic hall involving NZ $4 million.

Christchurch Airport is an attractive and busy New Zealand airport today, situated near the sprawling Canterbury Plains and overlooked by the majestic Southern Alps. The airport is just six miles from the centre of the city of Christchurch and 15 miles from the deep water port of Lyttelton. Facing the Pacific Ocean, this is among the world's most attractive airport locations.

Owned by the City Council, the airport is managed by the Christchurch Airport Authority, while the Civil Aviation Division of the New Zealand Ministry of Transport is responsible for the airport operations. As part of this responsibility the MOT provides ATC, communications and telecommunications engineering, fire and rescue, security, meteorological, and airworthiness services at the airport.

While modest in size by comparison with some of Europe's airports, Christchurch is also an important centre for local industry and employs almost 3,000 people at the airport alone. Apart from Air New Zealand, Mount Cook Airlines and Safe Air, there are

Above: Serving the South Island of New Zealand, Christchurch International Airport is one of New Zealand's busiest, and has a history of flying dating from pre-World War I. The airport is an employment hub for numerous companies.

facilities for QANTAS and the former domestic operator National Airways Corporation, as well as numerous other companies including Air Foods NZ Limited, a meat processing company which air freights frozen meat overseas. The Royal New Zealand Air Force uses Christchurch, while the Canterbury Aero Club flourishes, and recently celebrated its 50th anniversary.

For airline travellers there are the usual facilities including airport shops and a duty-free store. There are hairdressing salons open six days a week, executive rooms for press conferences and business meetings, and an airport hotel in the form of the White Heron Travelodge. This has 112 rooms and a swimming pool.

For the future, a new international terminal is under construction, and Stage One of this will be completed in 1980. This is expected to satisfy traffic requirements until about 1986, when Stage Two will be built. Runway extension work planned will lengthen the main runway to almost 10,000ft (3,000m).

43

Cologne-Bonn

West Germany

Location: 7 miles from Cologne and 15 miles from Bonn
Elevation: 295ft (90m)
Runways in use: 3
14L/32R 12,464ft × 200ft (3,800m × 60m)
14R/32L 6,120ft × 165ft (1,866m × 50m)
07/25 8,066ft × 150ft (2,459m × 45m)
Airport area: 2,470 acres
Passengers handled in 1977: 1,991,590
Total aircraft movements in 1977: 76,131
Cargo handled in 1977: 77,354 tons

The Federal German Republic must be given credit for establishing a system of airports which successfully serves all of the major cities in the country, and these airports have been brought to an advanced state, both constructionally and operationally, in the past few years.

Cologne-Bonn Airport is one of these modern airports, and is attractive both in its style and location, just seven miles from Cologne and 15 miles from the Federal capital of Bonn. The airport started life as an airfield for the Luftwaffe in 1938, at a location known as the Wahner Heide. It was enlarged somewhat by the occupying forces in the period 1945-50, and then first discussions about providing a civil airport to serve both Cologne and the newly designated Federal capital of Bonn were held in 1949. In 1950 approval was given for the development of the civil airport, and it was arranged that the principal shareholders in the operating company should be the German Federal Republic, and Land of North Rhine-Westphalia, and the cities of Cologne and Bonn.

Below: *Cologne-Bonn Airport will ultimately have four star-shaped terminal buildings joined to the main terminal, as traffic requires. The airport serves the Federal German capital as well as the important city of Cologne.*

On 1 February 1951 the airport was transferred to German administration, and the unfolding story of growth to great strength commenced. When West Germany's own airline, Deutsche Lufthansa, began postwar operations in 1955, the airport began to play an increasingly important role.

A programme of development began in 1958 to bring the airport up to international standard, and in 1970 the inauguration of the new terminal, on 20 March, saw the completion of the work. Today, the interesting arrangement of the airport provides for drive-in facilities, where cars or buses may be taken straight to the terminal buildings on specially constructed roads, to deposit their passengers at concrete, steel and glass buildings for check-in.

This check-in is performed through a decentralised system, which abandoned the usual idea of a large central hall with rows of ticket counters in favour of a terminal building with two star-shaped satellite buildings each containing six check-in counters. Under the first section of the project, there are two satellites linked to the main horseshoe-shaped building, but with ultimate realisation of the plan there will be four in all, disposed around the main building. The main terminal itself has six floors and its wings have four. The departure level for passengers is on the first floor, and they exit from the satellites to the aircraft by way of airbridges. The check-in units are directly related to individual aircraft positions, thus only passengers for the same destination assemble together, and domestic and international flights are handled under the arrangement without conflict.

The satellites also admit arriving passengers, who make their way by the airbridges to the main building where they finally arrive at ground level by way of stairs and escalators, reclaiming their baggage in the process.

The present capacity of the airport is approximately three million passengers a year. When it has reached that capacity the two extra star terminals will be added.

Copenhagen (Kastrup)   Denmark

Location: 5 miles SSE of Copenhagen
Elevation: 17ft (5m)
Runways in use: 3
04L/22R 11,800ft × 150ft (3,600m × 45m)
04R/22L 10,825ft × 150ft (3,300m × 45m)
12/30 9,184ft × 150ft (2,800m × 45m)
Airport area: 2,583 acres
Passengers handled in 1977: 8,471,800
Total aircraft movements in 1977: 163,800
Cargo handled in 1977: 156,300 tonnes

The big question mark hanging over Copenhagen Airport for the past few years has concerned the development of Saltholm. The island of Saltholm lies in the sound between Denmark and Sweden and has been uninhabited except by birds. It was decided in 1968 that Saltholm was the best possible site for an airport which could provide for growing traffic in Scandinavia and which could replace Kastrup. Kastrup had served Denmark well as its international gateway, but was size-limited.

When the remarkable growth in traffic of the 1960s and early 1970s slowed, a reappraisal was given to the Saltholm Airport project. While Saltholm offered much from the environmental standpoint, the cost of developing this site would clearly be astronomical, and it appeared that such an airport might not be needed after all — at least until the end of the century, by which time aircraft might be quite different in form and operational character.

The seal was set on the Saltholm idea in June 1978 with the report to the Copenhagen Airports Authority by the committee set up to investigate conclusively the scheme. The Copenhagen Airport Committee of 1975 ruled, with its report, that the Saltholm project should not be proceeded with. In other words, the Saltholm island airport was 'dead' — at least for a good many years to come.

Kastrup, it was decided, should remain the international airport for Copenhagen, for a number of reasons. For one, it would be much cheaper to extend Kastrup than move to Saltholm. The rate of growth in traffic at Kastrup suggested that the present airport would still be able to cope with the passenger throughput up to the end of the century, and, moreover, the capacity of the main runway system would be sufficient for the amount of traffic expected up to the year 2000. For capacity purposes, in fact, there would be no need to alter the runway system. It would be possible to make extensions to the terminal buildings and aircraft handling stands within the existing airport boundaries.

Kastrup, then, will go on serving Denmark's capital city in the way it has done since it was opened over 50 years ago, on 20 April 1925. It has undergone many changes since that date, and will undoubtedly undergo more, but its familiar and friendly form will continue to greet passengers passing through, for this is the prime international hub for Scandinavian traffic. The three-nation air partnership representing Norway, Denmark and Sweden in the form of the national carrier Scandinavian Airlines System (SAS) regards Kastrup as its principal operational base, and, amongst other things, has its air cargo terminal at the airport.

From the 5,000 passengers that used Copenhagen Airport in 1925, traffic is now up to the 8½ million travellers annually. It is expected to be of the order of 22 million by the year 2000, when further changes will have been made to the terminals; the present international terminal can be extended eastwards as well as westwards.

Below: *Copenhagen's Kastrup Airport, which will serve the city until the year 2000 at least.*

Curaçao International (Dr Albert Plesman)

Netherlands Antilles

Location: 5 miles NW of Willemstad, Curaçao
Elevation: 27ft (8m)
Runways in use: 1
11/29 11,150ft × 200ft (3,400m × 60m)
Passengers handled in 1977: 956,254
Total aircraft movements in 1977: 41,426
Cargo handled in 1977: 7,429 tons

The presence of busy air transport hubs in distant parts of the world owes much to aviation pioneers who recognised the incredible possibilities for world airline services at the dawn of civil flying. Territorial interests had much to do with the matter also, for the small country of Holland had colonies in the 1920s in the Far East and in the western hemisphere, in Batavia or what is now known as Indonesia, and in the Caribbean in what is still known as the Netherlands Antilles.

Dr Albert Plesman founded KLM Royal Dutch Airlines in 1920 and soon turned his attentions to serving the group of six islands comprising the Netherlands Antilles, located just off the coast of Venezuela. When KLM introduced services to these islands, which were then Dutch territory, the need for a proper airport was established, and that airport today is named after the founder of KLM.

Curaçao International is one of the oldest airports in the Caribbean, and is the gateway to Curaçao and its capital city, Willemstad. It is strategically located 38 miles to the north of Venezuela and, apart from tourist traffic which has grown as these islands have become recognised as attractive ports-of-call for holiday visitors, has grown in importance over the years, firstly because of its importance in the chain of Allied air bases in World War II, and secondly because Curaçao is now the site of one of the world's largest Shell oil refineries.

The airport was first constructed in 1929 and, in view of the fact that the island is composed primarily of coral and hard volcanic rock, this construction task was no small undertaking for the time. The war years saw development, with the landing strip turned into a paved, lighted runway, and with commercial air services resumed after the war, traffic soon began to swell. Since then the runway has been lengthened and improved further, and the terminal facilities expanded to accommodate traffic brought firstly by the subsonic narrow-bodied jets, then the Jumbos, and then the Concorde. The single runway has also served the heavyweight C5A Galaxy, and can now accommodate any aircraft operating. Because of the ever-present Trade Wind blowing from the east at an average speed of 16 knots, only the one runway is required.

Passenger growth over the last 10 years has required the construction of a new annexe to the terminal building for processing outbound passengers, and another annexe for arriving passengers; conversion of the original building to a transit lounge, the erection of a new control tower

Below: Just a few minutes' flying time from the coast of Venezuela, is the impressive airport of Dr Albert Plesman, otherwise known as Curaçao International.

and a new air cargo warehouse. Resident airline ALM (in which KLM still has an interest) has also built a new hangar for its DC-9 fleet. A new road system serving the terminal, and associated parking lot for 650 vehicles, were completed in early 1978.

Navigational facilities have been similarly improved. The original NDB and VOR sites have been changed, and with the VOR re-location, a DME was added. Because of the proximity of the sea to the runway, the conditions at the airport are highly corrosive, and all runway and taxiway light circuiting was renewed in 1976. This project also included the installation of pavement approach lights; a new ILS system was introduced into service in January 1977. New surveillance and approach control radars were also made operational in January 1977.

Because of air transport Curaçao is no longer an island outpost. The mainland of South America is a few minutes away and the United States and Holland are 2½hr and 8hr away respectively. Today, 96% of the people visiting the island arrive by way of the airport, and many perishable commodities previously unknown on the island are airfreighted in as a matter of course.

From mid-1978 Dr Albert Plesman Airport was divorced from government operation to become an autonomous body, operated and managed by an independent company.

Dallas-Fort Worth   USA

Location: 17 miles from both Dallas and Fort Worth, Texas
Elevation: 596ft (179m)
Runways in use: 3
17R/35L 11,400ft × 200ft (3,474m × 60m)
17L/35R 11,400ft × 200ft (3,474m × 60m)
13L/31R 9,000ft × 200ft (2,743m × 60m)
Airport area: 17,500 acres
Passengers handled in 1977: 17,318,726
Total air transport movements in 1977: 320,000
Cargo handled in 1977: 88,234 tons

One of the most remarkable airports that has been brought into being in the last five years is Dallas-Fort Worth, which typifies the American approach to building on a grand scale but which could well be one of the last really big airports to be constructed in the world. While the airport does not occupy all of the land allocated to its site, this site covers 17,500 acres; centres of population in most countries of the world no longer have such areas readily available for development.

While the airport is new in operational terms, its history is long and in fact goes back to 1927. In that year the city of Fort Worth, Texas, moved into commercial aviation with the construction of Meacham Field. Discussions were held with Dallas about the idea of a regional field to serve both cities, but the talks came to nothing and Dallas then gained its own airport with the purchase of the US army airfield, Love Field, in 1928. In 1940 both cities asked the Civil Aeronautics Administration for help to expand their airports and again the question was raised of developing a combined regional facility, but again the talks dragged on and in the meanwhile both Love Field and Fort Worth airports were independently developed. In May 1961, however, the Federal Government indicated it would like to see the two cities cooperate on a single airport, and the Civil Aeronautics Board and FAA supported the concept of a regional airport. In 1965, after more months of discussion the Dallas-Fort Worth Regional Airport Board was organised, and that year the Texas Legislature approved the creation of an authority to govern a new airport. In April 1968 funding and the planning and construction of the new airport were authorised and ground-breaking ceremonies began in December 1968. Drainage work on the site began in January 1969 and five years later, to the month, the airport opened for business.

Apart from its size, the notable thing about Dallas-Fort Worth is that it is built literally between the two cities, 17 miles from the central business districts of both, and serves the two Texas communities primarily. It is, of course, designed as an international airport, and in the few short years that it has been operational has demonstrated its importance to the American air transport business by becoming the fourth busiest airport in the USA in terms of air transport movements.

As the illustrations show, Dallas-Fort Worth is not only big but it is a good-looking airport embodying advanced ideas, and it is interesting to know that in arriving at the design the airport's planners made use of computer simulation studies to determine the airspace demands and then requirements for airport growth. From these came the concept of a multi-terminal facility served by a central, spine road, and flanked by long parallel runways for simultaneous take-offs and landings. The master plan for the airport was based on airspace demands for up to 178 aircraft movements an hour under instrument flight rules, or, in fact, near saturation conditions. To handle this number of aircraft, 11 runways were built into the master plan and as many as 13 terminals. In true Texas tradition, Dallas-Fort Worth was made big, and much bigger than is actually required at the present.

For the moment at least, the airport has four terminals and three runways, two of which are the north-south parallel runways, 11,400ft long and 200ft wide, and the third runway being a cross-wind runway of 9,000ft length. As with all of the runways planned, the present strips will handle aircraft weighing up to 800 tons and are fully equipped with instrument landing systems for Category II operations.

The terminals offer 66 boarding gates and are used at the moment by three international airlines, eight domestic carriers and five commuter operators. The terminal structures are semi-circular in design and based on the 'drive-to-gate' concept, which means that a minimum amount of distance for walking is required of the traveller from the point where he parks his car, on the landside of the terminal, to the point where he boards his aeroplane. The concept is followed throughout the airport and

47

Left: One of the semicircular terminal areas at Dallas-Fort Worth, which provide basic facilities for passengers while involving a minimum walking distance from the car parks.

Bottom left: Dallas-Fort Worth Airport is unique in that it was built specifically to serve the two named cities of Texas and is located almost equidistant between their business centres. The central, spine road is flanked by the semicircular terminal areas and which, in turn, are adjoined by the parallel runways.

the individual terminal areas are reached by the International Parkway spine road and which connects at either end with state highways, 183 on the south and State Highway 114 at the north.

For moving between various points on the airport there is an Airtrans system, and this electrically-powered automatic transit system moves passengers and employees from terminal to terminal and to and from remote parking areas as required. The Airtrans system, made by the Vought Corporation, is a permanently operating 'people-moving' system which has a special place at big airports and which is seeing increasing use as a safe and efficient method of movement. Airtrans at Dallas-Fort Worth consists of 51 passenger vehicles, each of which carries up to 40 people. In the first three years of operation at DFW Airtrans carried 10 million riders.

In financial terms Dallas-Fort Worth Airport is already regarded as a good servant to its communities, returning to its master over $350 million annually. The activity at the airport generates more than $137 million annually through the purchase of supplies, goods and services, and this in itself gives direct economic benefit to the many hundreds of businesses and thousands of individuals in the region. Some 43,000 people are now said to be earning all or part of their livelihood from Dallas-Fort Worth.

Damascus International

Syria

Location: 14 miles SE of Damascus
Elevation: 2,020ft (616m)
Runways in use: 2
05R/23L 11,811ft × 150ft (3,600m × 45m)
05L/23R 8,860ft × 150ft (2,700m × 45m)
Passengers handled in 1977: 970,808
Total aircraft movements in 1977: 18,988
Cargo handled in 1977: 60,998 tons

The Syrians say, quite rightly, that Damascus is one of the most ancient cities in history, and this busy Middle-Eastern crossroads certainly has an atmosphere of the past which is strongly impressed upon the visitor. Situated at the eastern end of the Mediterranean, between Turkey, Jordan and Iraq, Syria is an important gateway to the Middle East, and its capital city deserving of a good international airport.

The new airport for Damascus was built over the period 1965-69 following a study made in 1955 which concluded that a new airport should be built to replace the original airport at Mezze. Mezze had been functioning for many years as the airport serving Damascus, but was quite unsuited for jet operations. The site for the new airport was determined by a German planning team, the Becker Institute, the final outcome of which was the location of the airport at the favoured site of Jdaidat El Khass, 14 miles from the city centre. While a good taxi ride from the city (the usual medium of transport for passengers) the site offered unimpeded take-off and landing prospects well away from hills, good drainage qualities of the soil, and excellent bearing characteristics of this soil for heavy aircraft. Now the prime international airport for Damascus, the airport at Jdaidat El Khass is situated ESE of the city between the towns of Rhassole and Jdaidat El Khass, and at an elevation of 2,020ft.

Unfortunately, construction of the beautiful terminal building had a chequered career, for while work began on this in 1970, its completion was deferred when costs escalated, and only in 1974 was further work done on bringing the design up to date. In July 1976 the Syrian Government awarded a contract for completion of the terminal to a Syrian firm, the General Company for Building of Damascus, to impress the terminal into service speedily. On a recent visit by the author, however, this fine passenger terminal had still to be completely finished and it was giving way to the adjoining freight terminal, which had been converted into the passenger building pending completion of the passenger terminal proper.

The new Damascus International Airport is an elegant and well laid-out facility designed for the processing of two million or more passengers a year. It has two runways, parking space for up to 16 big jets on the apron within walking distance of the terminals, and is an impressive aerial gateway to the Syrian Arab Republic. A slender, 138ft high control tower oversees the runways, which are equipped with Category II ILS. VOR and DME aids are available, together with VHF and Tropilog receivers.

Damascus Airport is the location for the air traffic control centre for the Damascus Flight Information Region, and which covers airspace extending over Syria, Jordan and the northern part of Saudi Arabia. The parallel runways offer up to 11,800ft length.

Below: Control tower at the new airport for Damascus.

Dubai International   UAE

Location: 3 miles east of Dubai city
Elevation: 24ft (7m)
Runways in use: 1
12/30 13,880ft × 150ft (4,230m × 45m)
Passengers handled in 1977: 1,139,552
Total aircraft movements in 1977: 47,000
Cargo handled in 1977: 34,600 tons

There are seven states in the United Arab Emirates; Dubai is one, of them and has perhaps one of the best-looking airports in the region. It does not come entirely from new-found oil wealth, for the British firm of constructors Richard Costain Limited created this in 1971, to a contract valued at £4 million, but as with all airports in the Gulf and UAE much of the new-found affluence has been turned into the latest aids and equipment, to the benefit of users and operators alike.

Dubai is putting much into its economy to improve the standards of living of its citizens and an increasing number of visitors, and much effort is going into diversifying industrial and commercial development to make the region less dependent upon oil in the years ahead. It is a major objective, for example, to make the UAE self-sufficient in food, and for this reason agricultural procedures are being modernised. In Dubai itself a dry dock capable of accommodating super tankers is being built, and a satellite communications centre has been

Below: *The elegant lines of Dubai Airport, UAE, typify architectural features representative of the Middle East, although the airport terminal was built by the British firm of Costain.*

concentrated at Jebel Ali, near Dubai, to provide international telephone, telex, high-speed data and colour television transmission facilities. A Dubai trade centre has also been built.

All of this activity has been manifest to a large degree in passenger and cargo traffic increases through the airport, and some of the figures recording this situation are quite remarkable. It should be noted that the cost of air freight has been of relatively minor significance to those on the receiving end, and for this reason all kinds of commodities, products and materials have been airfreighted in. When the sea port at Port Rashid became congested with ships the airport took on even more work as shippers turned to the air. The closure of Beirut Airport in 1976 imposed yet a further strain on Dubai, with one airline, all-freight operator Trans-Mediterranean Airways, moving its complete operation to the airport.

The result of all of these factors has been to produce traffic figures which show increases of several hundred per cent. In 1972, for example, 6,880 tons of cargo were moved through Dubai Airport. In 1975 the loaded and unloaded total was 15,000 tons. In terms of passenger traffic there was an increase from 63,000 passengers to 85,600 passengers in the period from April 1976 to August 1976. In August 1976, after TMA moved the bulk of its fleet and equipoment to Dubai, cargo traffic figures showed an increase in cargo throughput of no less than 623% over the August of 1975.

However, this situation has been changing in recent times with the return to Beirut by TMA and the elimination of congestion at the seaport of Rashid, and in 1977 freight figures for Dubai

International fell markedly — for outgoing cargo by no less than 73%. Total air freight handled in 1977 was 34,600 tons compared with 51,885 tons in 1976. Passenger traffic is still rising, however, and in 1977, totalled 1,139,552, compared with 901,732 in 1976. It is expected that this trend will continue, with both cargo and passenger traffic growing at slower rates from here on.

The airport terminal facilities have been considerably enlarged and modernised in the last few years for the 40 scheduled and non-scheduled operators that use the airport, and the government recently allocated Dirham 800 million for further work. This work includes construction of a second runway and a new terminal. The present facilities are certainly capable of handling the current traffic, but the astonishing growth rates that have been experienced have led the authorities, wisely, to prepare for substantial future growth.

It is by no means certain that Dubai will see such massive traffic, however, for an abundance of airports has been built in the Gulf in recent times and more have been planned. Just 12 miles from Dubai is Sharjah Airport, and to the north at Ras Al Khaimah a new airport was opened in March 1976. Yet another airport near Dubai, at Jebel Ali, 17 miles to the south-west, has been planned, but it is now thought that this airport may not be built after all. With further enlargement of Dubai already in hand it may not be needed.

Dusseldorf

West Germany

Location: 4 miles north of Dusseldorf
Elevation: 144ft (44m)
Runways in use: 2
06/24 9,840ft x 150ft (3,000m x 45m)
16/34 5,347ft x 165ft (1,630m x 50m)
Passengers handled in 1977: 5,809,218
Total aircraft movements in 1977: 111,035
Cargo handled in 1977: 39,164 tons

Like so many of the airports in Germany, Dusseldorf was first activated as a flying field by the use of airships, and in September 1909 the first Zeppelin paid a call to what was later to become an airship base. In 1912 the Zeppelin *Schwaben* was housed at the site, and by 1913 these aerial giants were joined by the first biplanes.

It was not until 1927, however, that the site north of the city and just a few kilometres from the River Rhine saw its first duty as an airport, when in April 1927 the first airline services began by the forerunner of the present Lufthansa. The succeeding years saw a range of now-historic types of aircraft use the airport with bigger and heavier passenger loads, and among them was the Junkers F13, said to be the world's first all-metal civil aeroplane and of which type Lufthansa once owned 50 aircraft. The F13 was followed by types such as the Messerschmitt M18, the M20, the Dornier *Merkur* and the giant Junkers G38.

As the aircraft grew, so did the airport, until the time of World War II when it was taken over for military purposes. By now the city's airport had an attractive clutch of buildings, a spacious flying field

Below: *Passenger loading bridges in use at Dusseldorf, serving aircraft from both sides.*

Above: *Dusseldorf Airport is just over 50 years old, although this terminal design has been brought into being over the last 10 years. When complete, the terminal wing building on the south side will match that to the north.*

which had been used regularly by numerous international airlines, and an open air restaurant which attracted many visitors in the summer months.

The first postwar services were made to the rebuilt airport in April 1949 when British European Airways began a service from Northolt and linking Hamburg. Scandinavian Airlines followed with services between Dusseldorf and Copenhagen, and KLM, SABENA and Air France then joined them. US operators American Overseas Airlines and Pan American introduced services in September 1950.

With the commencement of services by the reborn Lufthansa in 1955, Dusseldorf once again began to take its place as a German air transport facility, and like its national airline, has been expanding steadily ever since. It was not until the 1960s however, that a new terminal development scheme and airport expansion programme got under way, and this terminal development programme is still in train, on a phased basis.

A number of design ideas had been drawn up in the 1950s, one of these, in 1952, providing for a long, single terminal in the centre of two parallel runways, and which would have provided parking places for aircraft on either side and under a canopied roof after the fashion of Berlin's famous Tempelhof Airport, now closed. Another design, conceived in 1955, envisaged a half-circle passenger

terminal with control tower on the inside of this circle. The design was interesting because it considered remoted square terminal buildings, spaced out over a very large apron against which individual aircraft parked. Passengers would have presumably reached these terminal halls by underground passageways from the main building.

These various designs were abandoned in favour of the present design, which has a central terminal building fronted by a trident-like complex of three piers, after the shape of a compressed W. Work on this design was put in hand in 1967, the airport's 40th anniversary year, and terminal construction work began in February 1969. The new central terminal was begun in May 1971. Under the first phase of this terminal scheme the central prong of the fork was built and the northerly pier, together with the main terminal structure and an adjoining multi-storey carpark building. The southerly pier will be built as traffic requirements dictate.

With the central pier surmounted by a circular, three-level control tower, the overall design is both attractive and interesting. Both the central apron and northerly pier areas provide parking spaces for no fewer than 22 large aircraft, at nose-in positions. These aircraft are served by articulated passenger airbridges linked to the terminals. Other parking places provide for a further 28 aircraft.

Dusseldorf Airport celebrated its 50th anniversary in 1977, a year in which it handled 5,800,000 passengers and 111,000 aircraft movements, 31,000 of which were general aviation movements. A recent facility for passengers has been the introduction of a rail link, which takes travellers direct to the airport from the city centre.

East Midlands (Castle Donington)   UK

Location: 8 miles SE of Derby
Elevation: 310ft (94m)
Runways in use: 2
10/28 7,480ft × 150ft (2,280m × 45m)
01/19 2,900ft × 335ft (884m × 102m) (grass)
Passengers handled in 1977: 684,184
Total aircraft movements in 1977: 12,200
Cargo handled in 1977: 8,000 tons

One of the underrated airports of the United Kingdom is East Midlands Airport, which has been overshadowed by the larger airport of Birmingham, but which is a fine airport and one with great potential. The history of the airport goes back to the 1940s, when an RAF aerodrome was constructed at nearby Castle Donington. Prior to this, the city of Derby had its own airfield in the form of Derby Airport, which was originally built as an all-grass airfield. Such airlines as Derby Airways started life here, serving the Midlands region of Britain and places farther afield. When the cities of Derby, Leicester and Nottingham got together to take over the old aerodrome of RAF Castle Donington, this became the principal airport for Derby, superseding the original airport.

Located in a triangle formed by the cities of Derby, Leicester and Nottingham, East Midlands Airport, as it was renamed, is strategically situated to serve these important cities and others in the centre of England. It is just two miles from the M1 motorway and less than two hours' drive from London or Leeds. Birmingham, and other industrial areas in the West Midlands, and Sheffield are about one hour's drive away.

Since its take-over by the East Midlands Airport Joint Committee in the mid-1960s, substantial development work has taken place at the site, at first under a plan which covered the five year period to 1971, providing for expenditure of just under £2 million for terminal work and the extension of the single hard runway to 7,480ft. In 1973 a development study was produced by an independent consulting firm for further work, and this advocated further extension of the runway. This study, however, was based upon the probability of the development of Maplin Airport, and was overtaken by events. The Joint Committee has now drawn up a fresh plan for the 1980s which sees a passenger throughput of up to 1.5 million passengers a year at the existing facilities. In the light of the British Government's recently published Airport Policy document, East Midlands Airport will undoubtedly grow to handle very many more in the years to come, and could well be running at three million passengers a year by 1990.

Facilities for handling the traffic at the moment are good, and include an attractive and comfortable terminal, spacious car parks and a good restaurant. Some 32 national and international airlines are already using the airport and 33 inclusive tour operators have winter or summer programmes to 28 destinations outside mainland Britain from the airport. Scheduled services are operated from East Midlands Airport to Amsterdam, Brussels, Frankfurt, Paris, Dublin, Belfast, Glasgow and the Channel Islands by various carriers including KLM, Britannia Airways, Alitalia, British Caledonian and British Midland Airways — which began life as Derby Airways and as the airport's 'own' operator has grown to a jet airline with a fleet of DC-9s.

While 50% of the traffic at the airport is currently holiday traffic, East Midlands is also becoming a major air freight centre. The airport has two cargo terminals, and handled 8,000 tons of cargo in 1977.

To provide for future traffic, application has been made for the runway to be extended to 9,491ft (2,893m). This would give the airport a capability for handling wide-bodied jets, including the B747. The cost of this runway extension could be borne by income from additional movements and by the increased revenue from handling, parking charges and concessions.

Below: East Midlands Airport, situated in the heart of England, has potential for future traffic of up to three million passengers a year.

Edinburgh (Turnhouse)   UK

Location: 7 miles west of Edinburgh, Scotland
Elevation: 135 ft (41m)
Runways in use: 3
07/25 8,400ft × 150ft (2,560m × 45m)
13/31 6,000ft × 150ft (1,829m × 45m)
08/26 3,455ft × 150ft (1,053m × 45m)
Airport area: 901 acres
Passengers handled in 1977: 1,021,600
Total aircraft movements in 1977: 20,600
Cargo handled in 1977: 1,300 tonnes

Scotland's principal city gained a new airport on
27 May 1977 when the redeveloped airport at
Turnhouse was put into commission with a spanking
new terminal and runway. The new terminal was
opened by HM the Queen, and this terminal is
designed to accommodate up to 1.5 million
passengers a year. The development work cost £15
million.

Below: *The new terminal at Edinburgh Airport was
opened by HM the Queen in May 1977, and will
provide for up to 1.5 million passengers a year. The
domestic wing is at the top of the picture, and shows
the proximity of the car park to the terminal and
aircraft.*

There has been an airfield at Turnhouse since
1915, when the Royal Flying Corps used the base for
training, and the field remained an air force site until
1960, when RAF Fighter Command handed over
control to the Ministry of Civil Aviation. It was,
however, already seeing commercial air services, for
British European Airways used it from 1947, and air
transport operations were carried on progressively
through the 1950s. The main runway was extended
and strengthened, and a new terminal was built in
1956.

This terminal was subsequently enlarged, but the
airport facilities in general were inadequate for the
significant growth experienced in the late 1950s and
early 1960s, and further development was clearly
needed. Lengthy negotiation between the
Government, Edinburgh Corporation and the British
Airports Authority led to the transfer of ownership to
the BAA in April 1971. The conditions of this transfer
included a government grant to cover 75% of the
cost of a new runway and terminal complex to meet
future needs, and it is this development which has
just recently been completed. The new runway was
opened in April 1976, and it joins two others, which
between them are now handling 21,000 movements
a year.

Frankfurt (Rhein/Main)

West Germany

Location: 5 miles SW of Frankfurt
Elevation: 568ft (173m)
Runways in use: 2
07L/25R 12,792ft × 200ft (3,900m × 60m)
07R/25L 12,300ft × 150ft (3,750m × 45m)
Airport area: 2,982 acres
Passengers handled in 1977: 14,969,000
Total air transport movements in 1977: 201,765
Cargo handled in 1977: 541,000 tons

Plans for flying from what was to become the great Frankfurt Airport were first laid in 1924, when on 2 July the predecessor of the present Flughafen Frankfurt/Main AG (Frankfurt/Main Airport Company) was founded. This company was called Sudwestdeutsche Luftverkehrs (SWL), and the intitial capital was some DM 400,000. The aim of the company was the promotion of public aviation and the construction of airports and airship terminals, an ambitious philosophy for the time, but one which seems to have reflected much foresight; one of the most active international airport planning and engineering consultancies today is Flughafen Frankfurt AG.

In the 1930s Frankfurt was the site of numerous Zeppelin operations and the Luftschiffbau Zeppelin GmbH was based there. In 1934 and 1935 greater attention was given to the German airships than to fixed-wing aeroplanes, for at that time the large ocean-ranging gas-filled Zeppelins seemed to hold greater promise for international flights than did the aeroplane. After a number of airship disasters, however, the aeroplane took over and Frankfurt became an aerodrome for aeroplanes alone.

In 1935 work began on the construction of the Rhein/Main airport, on the site occupied by the airport today. Then it occupied 1,580 acres, however, and now it covers 2,982 acres. On 8 July 1936 a Junkers Ju52 of Deutsche Lufthansa landed at the airport and this signalled the commencement of airliner flights. In the summer of 1937 27 destinations could be reached from Frankfurt Airport, and the number was expanding steadily. The war stopped commercial air services, however, and it was not until May 1945, when American troops took over the airfield, that a programme of rebuilding was begun to turn the site once again into a commercial airport.

Below: *Passenger terminal complex at Frankfurt/Main Airport, now one of the busiest in Europe. There are parking positions for 36 aircraft.*

Above: *Control tower structure at Frankfurt/Main.*

On 18 May 1946 an aircraft of American Overseas Airlines became the first civil transport to land at Frankfurt since the war, and three months later SAS commenced the first scheduled service, covering Copehagen to Marseilles by way of Frankfurt. Two years later, in 1948, the importance of the airport grew with the operation of the Berlin Airlift, and later this importance was strengthened when the world's first jet airliner, the Comet 1, entered service, for the first hard runways that had been laid were now a necessity.

In February 1950 the airport had been given the new official name of Frankfurt Rhein/Main Airport, and the first development work to expand the facility into a major air transport hub was carried out. This development programme culminated in a massive scheme for transforming the airport, which was begun in the 1960s with the construction of a new arrivals and departures building. A feature of this was a new domestic traffic lounge, in 1963, and then in 1964 a large-scale fuel storage facility was erected. In 1965 the foundation stone for the new central terminal was laid, and this was to be put into service in March 1972, after one of the largest construction programmes in the Federal German Republic.

Deutsche Lufthansa, once again one of the world's major airlines, has extensive facilities at Frankfurt, including its cargo headquarters, where a new automated cargo terminal has been built. Because of this work, and because Frankfurt is the main gateway airport to the Federal Republic, it has become the busiest cargo airport in Europe. From the passenger viewpoint Frankfurt/Main is now equipped to handle over 30 million passengers a year. While not one of the world's most attractive airports, it is certainly one of the most important.

Gatwick

UK

Location: 28 miles south of London
Elevation 194ft (59m)
Runways in use: 1
08/26 10,165ft x 150ft (3,098m x 45m)
Airport area: 14,498 acres
Passengers handled in 1977: 6,652,336
Total aircraft movements in 1977: 84,443
Cargo handled in 1977: 100,405 tons

If terminal facilities were the criteria for an airport to become established as an international air hub, Gatwick would be accepted the world over, for with the recent completion of a £100 million Stage III development scheme the airport can match the best of such airports on six continents. Equally, the traffic at this London airport is already respectable in international terms, although the British Government would like to see its annual throughput being greater, taking some of the pressure off over-crowded London Heathrow. Currently handling almost seven million passengers a year, the new facilities at Gatwick have a capacity for 16 million and an ultimate capacity of 25 million.

Gatwick began life as a private aerodrome in August 1930 on a site about a mile south of the present terminal. In 1934 the first public licence was issued to the operators, a company called Airports Limited, and the first moves toward development were made. The first development scheme included the construction of a circular terminal known as the Beehive, and the airport managers introduced the novel idea of having the airliners of the day taxi up to this building and park around it at designated places. Passengers reached the aircraft by walking through one of the six short covered walkways, a concept which might be said to have been the first pier system functioning from a radial terminal in England, and possibly Europe.

In this form the airport was officially opened for air transport flights on 6 June 1936 by the Secretary of State for Air, Viscount Swinton. The war years saw Gatwick requisitioned by the Air Ministry, and in 1946 the RAF indicated that it would relinquish the use of the airport, but the de-requisitioning was deferred, and by June 1947 the Ministry of Civil Aviation had prepared a memorandum to the effect that Gatwick might be developed as a future London airport. As Heathrow had already been chosen as the principal London Airport, Gatwick's future remained uncertain.

By July 1952 announcement was made in Parliament of the Government's decision to develop Gatwick as an alternate to London Airport, and from then on the scene was set for a run-up to development of the airport according to a postwar Stage I scheme. Under this scheme a box-like terminal with a single 900ft long pier was built on a site to the north of the original Beehive (which still stands today), and a 7,000ft long runway laid.

This brand new airport, which cost under £7 million to build, was adequate until 1962, when Heathrow was already showing signs of strain from charter and holiday traffic. It was then decided to implement a Stage II scheme, which involved the construction of two more piers, laterally disposed to the terminal, and the expansion of the terminal building to about double its previous size. The runway was lengthened to 8,200ft and the apron doubled in area.

Recognising the potential of the airport in the wake of the fiasco over the creation of a third London airport, eventually abandoned, the Government planners approved a third development scheme, and in May 1974 the first phase of this work was completed with the construction of an international arrivals terminal. The first phase, which saw the installation of substantial advanced equipment, was followed by completion of the second phase eight months later. Under this work a brand new multi-storey car park was built on the other side of the main London railway line, which connects with the

Below: *Terminal buildings at Gatwick, from the airside.*

Overleaf: *Gatwick after completion of Stage III development scheme, mid-1978.*

Above: *The new pier at Gatwick Airport, 1,440ft long, or almost twice the length of the original 1958 pier. The north and south lateral piers may be rebuilt.*

airport, a new catering suite including a restaurant, banqueting area and cocktail lounge, and a linking bridge, equipped with Travelator, constructed to join the new car park to the main terminal.

This third stage of development was scheduled to cost £70 million, and provided for the later replacement of the original central pier by a new pier, equipped with moving walkways, airbridges and air conditioned gate rooms, and the construction of a new cargo centre to the north of the single runway. After expenditure of £100 million, Stage III was completed with the opening in November 1977 of the new central pier. This provides for 11 parking stands for wide-bodied aircraft, with provision for four more parking places on the apron. With the complementary north and south piers, parking stands in the terminal area are raised to some 27 in total.

With this development work passenger capacity at Gatwick has been raised to 16 million passengers/year. In its new form Gatwick is a fine

airport and very different to the charter-flight airport of the 1950s. The problem for the British Airports Authority, which owns and manages the airport, is to persuade airlines which use Heathrow to move to Gatwick and transfer some or all of their services to London's second airport. Fifteen international carriers already use the airport and more will undoubtedly join them, in the manner of Delta Air Lines and Braniff International, in mid-1978. Understandably, however, numerous other carriers which have traditionally used Heathrow have refused to move because of their investments at Heathrow and because of expected disruption of their flight schedules.

While this problem may be overcome in time, a more important reason for apprehension on the part of many airlines is the British Government's insistence on limiting the number of runways at the airport to one. It is felt by many that the handling of 160,000 air transport movements/year, which is the approximate number involved in carrying 25 million passengers through the airport, will be out of the question with a single runway. While a second runway for the airport was provided for in the Stage I scheme, this land has now been built over.

Geneva (Cointrin)   Switzerland

Location: 2.5 miles from Geneva city centre
Elevation: 1,410ft (430m)
Runways in use: 1
05/23 12,792ft × 164ft (3,900m × 50m)
Passengers handled in 1977: 3,790,800
Total aircraft movements in 1977: 68,600
Cargo handled in 1977: 34,700 tons

The efficiency of the Swiss is internationally recognised, and there are various manifestations of this efficiency in Swiss air transport, as exemplified by Swissair, the national airline, which moves cautiously but almost always does well annually, the KSSU partnership, of which Swissair was a prime mover, and the Swiss airport system, which effectively handles an important traffic while generally managing to overcome all of the noise, environmental and communications problems that might be expected in a small, high-income country such as Switzerland.

There are no more than half a dozen principal air transport airports in Switzerland, and Geneva is ranked second to Zurich amongst these in terms of passenger traffic and airline movements. Geneva-Cointrin is handling about 37% of all Swiss airport traffic, and with a throughput now of just under four million passengers annually it takes its place among the favoured European air ports of call.

The airport's efficiency was becoming stretched by 1965, when a growing tide of smaller airlines were using the airport every year on holiday charter flights, to the relief of Zurich and the further betterment of the Swiss economy, but to the mild anxiety of the airport authorities. They were aware that Cointrin was ill-equipped to handle big new aircraft that were on the drawing boards, should they become a reality (the Boeing 747 was ordered first in 1966).

It was in 1965, therefore, that the Geneva Cantonal authorities decided to institute a modernisation programme which would not only reshape the airport but which would be bold enough to provide for all kinds of aircraft and their traffic for a long time to come.

For Geneva Airport, this was not the first modernisation plan that had been implemented. The city of Geneva had had an airport since 1920, when an air route between Cointrin and Paris had been inaugurated, and in 1944 a new concrete runway was laid to prepare for the postwar traffic. The grass strip and wooden huts of 1922 gave way in 1945 to a postwar improvement scheme, but since that time there had not been a development programme of such magnitude — or cost.

The dramatic new plan of 1965 called for tunnels and a system of satellite terminals linked with the main terminal, to keep the apron clear for very large aircraft. The Geneva plan made obsolete the former terminal building, with its now-quaint arrangement for travellers to walk across the apron to board the aircraft — in any weather. A new system of roads was also required, together with a hydrant fuelling system, passenger conveyors and escalators, and clearly-defined direction flows. Most importantly, the satellite terminals would be unlike anything the airport had ever had before, and would, in fact, come to serve as a model design concept for many other international airports, although the last feature was not thought of greatly at the time.

Below: *Geneva Airport, showing main terminal and three satellite terminals, which connect with the main building by underground channel.*

Brought to reality in 1968 (two years before the Boeing 747 began operations), the Geneva plan introduced the first remoted satellite terminal system to any European airport. With this arrangement three radial terminals were positioned on the apron, some way from the main terminal by which passengers depart from the airport and make their way to Geneva and environs when arriving at it.

Below: The three main radial satellite terminals at Geneva are well removed from the main building, thereby providing an uncluttered apron for aircraft manoeuvring and producing improvements in the apron safety factor. A bonus is the improvement in aircraft noise level.

The radial satellites act as holding lounges for passengers after completing check-in and other procedures in the main terminal, and for the passenger the decision was generally quickly made to take the conveyor along the underground passageway to the terminal and his aircraft parked alongside it. The option is open to remain in the main terminal until departure time, but this is not easy if the traveller sees his aircraft taxi in — or believes he does. For the airport authority the satellite terminal idea was perfect insofar as it cleared the main terminal of languishing passengers to make more room for processing procedures.

Since the introduction of the system the traffic has doubled at Geneva-Cointrin and wide-bodied aircraft are regular callers at the airport, including the 747s and DC-10s of home carrier Swissair and the European Airbuses of other airlines.

Hamburg (Fuhlsbuttel)

Location: 5 miles north of Hamburg
Elevation: 52ft (16m)
Runways in use: 3
05/23 10,660ft x 150ft (3,250m x 45m)
16/34 12,020ft x 150ft (3,665m x 45m)
05/23 3,936ft x 165ft (1,200m x 50m) (grass)
Passengers handled in 1977: 3,995,055
Total aircraft movements in 1977: 29,392
Cargo handled in 1977: 35,424 tons

There has been flying at Hamburg, North Germany, since 1908, and while this flying began with balloons, such was the development of this form of aerial transport that airship hangars were established there in 1912, and the Graf Zeppelin operated from the airfield, which has been claimed to be 'the first airport in Europe'.

West Germany

Because of the importance of the city of Hamburg, Hamburg Airport became important too, and in the 1920s the national airline Lufthansa carried on many of its international services from there. Ths airport was later used for military purposes, and the postwar years then saw development of the site at Fuhlsubuttel, just five miles from the city, to the stature of the present day. Lufthansa has also made the airport its Technical Base, and amongst other things, the airline has aircraft overhaul and engine test facilities at the airport.

The terminal complex at Hamburg is after the traditional design of the prewar period, but this has of course undergone much modification in recent times. A curved central terminal looks out over a wide apron on which the aircraft are parked, and the terminal is fronted by a canopied structure beneath which passengers join their aircraft. Flanking the central terminal are two wing buildings which are provided with telescoping airbridges to support the traffic flow. The landside of the terminal is fronted by the Zeppelinstrasse, a main road passing the airport, and between this road and the terminal there is extensive car parking space. Such is the traffic at Hamburg that provision for long-term parking has been made on the other side of the Zeppelinstrasse also, to provide 1,827 open parking spaces in all. Some covered car parks are available also.

The airport is situated near the E3 Autobahn running to Flensburg and Kiel in the north and in the southerly direction to the suburbs of north-west Hamburg. To the south-west lies the city of Bremen, down the E3 Autobahn, and due south is Hanover. The airport thus plays a particularly important role in serving the north of the Federal German Republic, as well as Scandinavian countries.

Development plans for Hamburg Fuhlsbuttel were temporarily halted in 1968 when it was first announced that a new airport for Hamburg, located at Kaltenkirchen, further north of Hamburg and in the direction of Kiel, was to be built. This airport, a major project to cost many millions of DM, would have two half-circle terminal buildings, bisected by a main road, which would provide for all future big jets. Construction of the airport was deferred following the fuel crisis of 1973-74, and plans for the airport stretched out. Since that time, plans for the Kaltenkirchen Airport have been reactivated, and it is now thought likely that the airport could be introduced into service some time in the 1980s.

Below: *Claimed to be the first 'airport' in Europe, Hamburg was used for Zeppelin flights from 1912, but the first passenger buildings were not erected until the 1920s. This site, at Fuhlsbuttel, may be supplanted by a major new airport facility at Kaltenkirchen.*

Bottom: *Hamburg Airport is the major civil terminal in the Federal German Republic today, used by, amongst other aircraft, Lufthansa's A300 Airbus.*

Helsinki (Vantaa)   Finland

Location: 12 miles from Helsinki city centre
Elevation: 167ft (51m)
Runways in use: 2
04/22 10,500ft × 200ft (3,200m × 60m)
15/33 9,510ft × 200ft (2,900m × 60m)
Airport area: 2,965 acres
Passengers handled in 1977: 2,723,362
Total aircraft movements in 1977: 39,481
Cargo handled in 1977: 26,457 tons

The long, hard winters of countries in the northern latitudes give air transport authorities in those countries many problems, but the Finns have had long experience in meeting these problems for they have been carrying on air services for over 55 years. As the principal airport of Helsinki, Helsinki-Vantaa was opened in 1952 just prior to the Helsinki Olympic Games, and is now seeing traffic totalling almost three million passengers a year. This traffic has been climbing steadily over the years, but had a particular boost in the mid-1970s when national airline Finnair introduced its DC-9-50 and DC-10-30 aircraft on European and transatlantic services respectively.

The original landplane airport for Helsinki was at Malmi, opened in 1936, and prior to this date Katajanokka served as the base for seaplane operations, which were carried on right in the heart of the city. Malmi was superseded for international operations in 1952 with the opening of Vantaa Airport, which is further away from the city but purpose-built for big jet operations. Its location also ensures minimum noise nuisance.

Below: *Helsinki-Vantaa Airport is the busiest in Finland. The present terminal was brought into use in 1969, and is now handling almost three million passengers a year.*

The airport is situated in the province of Vantaa, near to the Tuusula Motorway and 12 miles from the Helsinki city centre. Apart from being the principal hub of commercial air traffic in Finland, the airport is also the centre for Finnish Air Traffic Control. It is also the home base for most Finnish air companies and most Finnish aviation concerns. National carrier Finnair has its headquarters, hangars and repair shops on the airport.

The present passenger terminal was brought into use in 1969. It serves both the scheduled domestic and international flights and charter services. The architects of Finland (notably Saarinen) have produced some elegant terminals for world airports and the terminal at Helsinki-Vantaa is no exception, with its sweeping roof and substantial areas of glass giving a wide aspect to the surrounding scene. For the traveller, warmth and light are welcome characteristics of the terminal, which is so constructed as to give a raised view of the apron. By its design the terminal is raised well above the apron level so that departing passengers may pass from elevated roadways straight through the terminal building and down into their aircraft cabins. The first level below the terminal on the landside is given over to airport buses and service vehicles for arriving passengers, while a second lower level is given over to a car park for airline passengers.

The airport has not yet moved to such advanced aids for winter operations as heated runways, but the Vantaa fleet of snowploughs and snow-dispersing equipment is substantial and ever-active in winter conditions, and the two runways are equipped for Category II bad weather landing operations. Both runways are equipped with low and high-intensity runway and approach lights, visual approach slope indicators and ILS facilities to ensure that the airport is constantly serviceable. Indeed, the airport authorities maintain that the airport is operational in all weather conditions, and traffic breaks have been restricted to 10 minutes at most.

Hong Kong (Kai Tak)

Location: Kowloon peninsula, 3 miles from Victoria
Elevation: 15ft (4.5m)
Runways in use: 1
13/31 11,130ft × 200ft (3,390m × 60m)
Passengers handled in 1977: 4,558,048
Total aircraft movements in 1977: 50,151
Cargo handled in 1977: 164,862 tons

The British Crown Colony of Hong Kong consists of 236 islands and islets and a portion of the Chinese mainland east of the Pearl River estuary. The total area of this land is 398¼ sq miles. The principal city of Hong Kong is Victoria, and facing Hong Kong Island is the Kowloon peninsular, where Kai Tak Airport is situated. Kowloon Bay is closely encircled on the landward side by high hills and the approaches over these to the airport are very poor. The mountainous nature of the region makes it a hazardous one for the airline pilots, and the idea of making long shallow approaches by big jets over this route is out of the question.

The city had an airport from 1929, when the newly formed Hong Kong Flying Club rented part of the land reclaimed from Kowloon Bay for its landing field. The field was developed into an airport, and by 1932 1,185 passengers had been flown from it. The Government then took over construction and operation of this site, and civil flying was put on to a money-making basis. In 1936 Imperial Airways began a weekly service between Hong Kong and Penang to connect with the England-Australia flights. By the end of the same year Pan American had opened another route, between Hong Kong and the United States, using flying-boats which landed on the waters of Kowloon Bay.

During World War II the airport was used by the Japanese as a strategic air base, and considerably enlarged. In the postwar period it was not until 1947 that the airport began to take its place in international air operations. It then had two runways, but their length and the general arrangement of the

site were considered limited, and after much discussion the Hong Kong Government decided that a completely new airport would have to be built on the existing site.

In 1954 work on this new airport was approved, and then began one of the biggest airport construction schemes undertaken in Asia. The principal feature of this project was the construction of the runway, for to overcome the problems caused by the surrounding mountains, it was to be built actually out into Kowloon Bay, stretching for 8,350ft from the mainland over the water. The project was a remarkable feat of engineering and construction work, and took 2½ years to complete. It involved the use of 20 million tons of material, including 11 million tons of filling, and the efforts of 3,000 workers daily. It cost the Hong Kong Government some $135 million, and was introduced into service in 1958.

Initially, this runway was made 8,350ft long and 200ft wide, and stressed to take aircraft weights of up to 450,000lb, but this length was extended to 10,000ft in the 1970s, when the first Boeing B747s began to operate.

Since this time, Kai Tak Airport has become even more important to international air transport as passenger traffic has increased from 1.5 to almost 5 million travellers a year, and substantial terminal expansion work has been required — and the runway lengthened yet again. A new terminal building was opened in November 1962, and an extension to the departures hall built in August 1977; a similar extension was made to the arrivals hall in early 1978.

Below: Kai Tak Airport terminal, Hong Kong, with 'resident' airline Cathay Pacific awaiting a new passenger load. The airport is handling almost five million passengers a year.

The passenger terminal is now handling more than 4,000 passengers an hour in peak periods, and to speed this traffic flow a semi-automatic baggage system, with computerised sorting, has been installed. The access roads to and from the airport have been improved, and the air traffic services provided with the latest equipment. An instrument landing system was commissioned in 1974, and secondary surveillance radar recently installed. In August 1977 a sequenced strobe lighting system was brought into operation to provide improved visual guidance at night and in poor visibility for landing aircraft.

With 26 international airlines providing 800 scheduled passenger services to and from Hong Kong each week, the single runway is now seeing a heavy annual utilisation, and by way of improving this runway further it was given additional length of up to 11,130ft, which became available at the end of 1975. Concurrently, construction was completed on a road tunnel under the north-west end of the runway. Such tunnelling work has benefited the movement of surface traffic to and from the airport and around it; the cross-harbour tunnel, which was opened in 1972, brought the airport to within a 15-minute drive of Hong Kong Island.

Apart from its passenger traffic, Kai Tak is one of the busiest cargo airports in Asia, and a new cargo complex was opened at the airport in 1976 with an ultimate handling capability of 500,000 tons. This cargo facility is financed and operated by Hong Kong Air Cargo Terminals Limited, a consortium comprising the Hong Kong Government and four local organisations.

As fascinating as it already is, the story of Kai Tak Airport may be taking a new turn, for indications are already being shown that the airport may become saturated for practical purposes by 1985. The next move would be a replacement airport for the Colony, and in order to provide for the possibility, studies are now in train on a new airport. One possible site for this would be the small island of Chek Lap Kok, off the north-west coast of Lantao Island and west of the Hong Kong mainland. A feasibility study for a new airport has now been put in hand.

Houston Intercontinental   USA

Location: 17 miles north of Houston city centre
Elevation: 98ft (30m)
Runways in use: 2
8L/26R 12,000ft × 150ft (3,658m × 45m)
14/32 9,400ft × 150ft (2,865m × 45m)
Airport area: 8,000 acres
Passengers handled in 1977: 7,996,935
Total aircraft movements in 1977: 240,497
Cargo handled in 1977: 56,881 tons

The world at large knows Houston, Texas, as the centre for Mission Control in the US space programme, and it is right therefore that the city has a space-age airport, imposing in its architecture and style. Houston has had an airport for many years, of course, since the 1920s, and the original facility started as a cow pasture to the south-east of the city. That grand facility was named the Municipal Airport, and was renamed the William P. Hobby Airport, after a local notable, in 1967 by which time a new airport for Houston was well into construction.

The first study to assess the city's future air transport needs was made in 1957, when big jet transports were on the horizon and Hobby Airport was acknowledged to be size-limited. Population and industry growth in Houston and the Texas Gulf Coast area was outpacing the development of air transport facilities, and the survey stressed the importance of the airport's keeping pace. A holding company called the Jet Era Ranch Company was founded as a medium through which 3,000 acres of land could be bought by a group of citizens of Houston for the sole purpose of resale to the city at the cost to them. This was the one way that accumulated land parcels could be acquired without long arguments over rights to oil or gas fields, highways, pipelines etc. In June 1960 the city council received full title to the 3,000 acres for development into a new airport. Additional land acquisitions, completed or in progress, then brought the total airport site to 7,300 acres. Ground-breaking began in 1962, and that year the Federal Aviation Administration selected Houston as the site for a major air route traffic control centre. The airport was officially opened for service on 1 June 1969 as Houston Intercontinental Airport. The old William P. Hobby Airport is still used as a Texas regional airport.

Houston Intercontinental is today handling eight million passengers a year from two runways and an initial two terminals. The two square-shaped terminals are positioned in the centre of a long, wide strip of land with concourses projecting from each corner. The concourses, which are in effect circular holding lounges with aircraft parking places around them, are linked to the main terminals by passenger bridges. The central strip of land is so laid out as to provide for a complete doubling in size of the whole facility, in a linear expansion plan. The master plan provides for this development, and the construction of a further two box terminals with their associate concourses. The central strip provides for car parking and the free movement of passengers through the terminal halls, to the restaurants and elsewhere. The apron is all around, and the central island is reached by subterranean driveways and an underground train. A $12 million hotel, the Host Hotel, is located in the centre of the terminal building complex.

There are two air cargo buildings at the airport with a third under construction. Construction of a third terminal is underway, with completion set for January 1981.

Istanbul (Yesilkoy) Turkey

Location: 15 miles west of Istanbul
Elevation: 92ft (28m)
Runways in use: 2
06/24 7,545ft x 200ft (2,300m x 60m)
18/36 9,840ft x 150ft (3,000m x 45m)
Passengers handled in 1977: 2,965,697
Total aircraft movements in 1977: 50,826
Cargo handled in 1977: 58,548 tons

Located in the heart of the Middle East between the Mediterranean and Black Seas, Turkey's geographical position is of great interest to business and tourist travellers alike. From a business point of view it represents an important hub at the eastern end of the Mediterranean, and for tourists the country holds cultural treasures representing a history which goes back thousands of years.

The two principal airports in the country are the capital city airport for Ankara (qv) and the airport for Istanbul, Yesilkoy. Of the two, Istanbul is by far the busiest handling twice the traffic annually of Ankara, and this airport is also the base for most foreign airlines serving Turkey together with national carrier Turkish Airlines (THY).

Yesilkoy was opened in 1953, and is a fairly sizeable airport designed in the conventional mould. It is located 15 miles from the city of Istanbul. It is currently seeing some 50,000 aircraft movements a year. A substantial amount of domestic airline traffic is flown within Turkey, and in the case of Yesilkoy, this domestic traffic is amounting to just under half of the total traffic handled — 1,200,000 passengers as against 1,700,000 international. Such busyness is a reflection of the preference for flying in this mountainous country.

The size of the airport, together with the climate have shaped the philosophy that passengers may walk across the apron to the parked aircraft without the need for boarding bridges. This apron at Yesilkoy has a capacity for three DC-10 and nine B707-types at one time.

For the future, Yesilkoy is to be given a brand new airport, which will have four terminal units eventually, each with a capacity for five million passengers a year. Terminal unit 1 is now under construction, for service about 1980.

Below: The busiest airport in Turkey is Istanbul, which is currently handling some 2.9 million travellers a year.

Jersey (Channel Islands) UK

Location: 6 miles WNW of St Helier
Elevation: 276ft (84m)
Runways in use: 1
09/27 5,595ft × 150ft (1,706m × 45m)
Airport area: 332 acres
Passengers handled in 1977: 1,420,354
Total aircraft movements in 1977: 53,673
Cargo handled in 1977: 11,314 tons

Above: *The most recent improvement to Jersey Airport, Channel Islands, has been the erection of a passenger pier, opened in March 1978. The airport is the third busiest in the UK in terms of aircraft movements annually.*

The Channel Islands airport of Jersey is an important one because of its great number of air transport movements every year. The airport has the greatest number of movements annually among all of the UK airports with the exception of the two London airports, Heathrow and Gatwick. The reason for this is the large volume of holiday traffic which flies in to the attractive island year-round and places the airport among the top six UK airports.

The first air services were run to Jersey from Portsmouth to the beach in St Aubins Bay in December 1933. Regular daily flights were made to this strip by Jersey Airways, but it was hardly the place for an airport proper to be established, and the Jersey Harbours and Airport Committee looked for and found a site where a good-sized airport could be developed. This was the present site, which is situated on the western side of the island and six miles from the principal town of St Helier. The airport is owned by the States of Jersey and administered by the Harbours and Airport Committee. The original airport had four runways, all of which were grass, and a terminal building was provided. In February 1940 a Fleet Air Arm training squadron was based at Jersey, but when the French Channel Ports were overrun commercial air services from the island stopped, and in July 1940 the island was occupied by the Luftwaffe and the airport came under its

command. From then on Jersey Airport was used by the Luftwaffe until the end of the war.

On 2 October 1945 the airport was handed back to the States of Jersey, and from then on, as the island's economy underwent a steady improvement, the airport began to see an ever rising traffic as a result of the popularity of air travel.

Various improvement works have been done at the airport in the succeeding years, culminating in the addition to the main terminal building of an international pier, which stretches across the apron to the south of the terminal building and control tower and which now provides for jet aircraft that until the mid-1960s were banned from using the airport. The new pier was opened in March 1978. Its erection had been accompanied by substantial enlargement of the apron, further lengthening of the main concrete runway to almost 6,000ft, the provision of additional hangar space and maintenance facilities, and installation of new navigational aids.

Today Jersey Airport is an important international facility and, in the peak periods between May and September, handles flights from Amsterdam, Berlin, Brussels, Rotterdam and Palma, as well as 14 places in France, Belfast and Dublin, and no fewer than 28 airports in Britain. On the busiest days in 1977 13,600 passengers were handled daily.

Kansas City International

USA

Location: 15 miles NW of Kansas City
Elevation: 1,027ft (313m)
Runways in use: 2
01/19 10,800ft × 150ft (3,294m × 45m)
09/27 9,500ft × 150ft (2,895m × 45m)
Airport area: 5,000 acres
Passengers handled in 1977: 4,655,093
Total air transport movements in 1977: 149,700
Cargo handled in 1977: 48,128 tons

An historic day for Kansas City, Missouri, was 17 August 1927 for on that day Colonel Charles A. Lindbergh flew into the airport that had just been built to officially dedicate it. Fresh from his Atlantic-crossing exploit, Lindbergh was in process of making a tour of the US continent for the promotion of aeronautics under a Guggenheim Foundation scheme. To the joy of thousands of spectators, the famous *Spirit of St Louis* circled for 15 minutes before touching down at the north end of the field.

Kansas had seen a fair amount of aviation long before this, however, for a balloon ascent was made from the heart of the city in 1869, and in 1917 the city opened its first 'airport' at a place called Holmes Road. Then in May 1926 the first airmail flight was made out of Kansas, from a place called Richards Field. By the 1940s the city in the heart of America's midwest had its own municipal airport, and with the foresight which appears to have characterised Kansas City's aviation thinking right from the start, it

Below: The striking and imaginative concept for Kansas City International is based upon that of ready car parking and a minimum of walking effort for the airline traveller. After leaving his car in the circular terminal park, he passes through the 65ft wide terminal building to the aircraft. Longer-term parking is available in the parks between the terminal sites.

was already considering the idea of a magnificent new international facility, designed to serve air transport for many years to come.

By the 1950s Kansas had committed itself to a second commercial airport and purchased some land for the purpose. Trans World Airlines located its main overhaul base at the eastern edge of this field, which became called Mid-Continent Airport (later Mid-Continent International). It was felt likely that this site would become the second airport, but by 1963 the inadequacy of Kansas City Municipal Airport indicated that a completely fresh development was required, and further land, therefore, was purchased adjacent to that originally acquired for purposes of a brand new international airport. This left TWA's base at the eastern end, with the planned airport site situated to the west.

The new airport came to be called Kansas City International, or KCI, and while it took no more than four years for the construction, its history proper began in 1963 with the decision by city officials that airline operations would have to be moved. When the plans were finalised, it was decided that 5,000 acres would be required for the airport, or some five times that of Municipal Airport. At that time, only two airports in the United States exceeded this size: New York International Airport and San Francisco International.

The concept of KCI was based on the facts that airline travellers in the main were usually obliged to leave their cars in a car park some distance from the terminal, trudge substantial distances to the check-in point, and then walk another 1,000 feet to board the aircraft. Planning for KCI dictated that irritations such as this should be eliminated as far as possible, and the idea was one of 'drive-to-your-gate', by which the traveller drove to the airport, followed signs indicating his flight number or direction, and parked virtually at the terminal entrance. Leaving his

car, the traveller accomplished baggage check-in in a matter of minutes, and by simply walking the width of a narrow building, could board the aircraft. At KCI the distance walked is not much more than 100ft.

To achieve this bold thinking the planners of KCI surrounded the circular control tower and airport administrative centre with four massive circular terminal complexes, like wheels around a larger central wheel. Each terminal complex provides a massive central parking lot with the narrow terminal building circling its edge. On the airside of this terminal 'wheel', is the apron on which the aircraft park. These aircraft are reached by passenger airbridges after the passenger has taken the appropriate gate for his flight.

The scheme might be compared with the traditional structural pier concept, which permits multiple loading of aircraft, but it is unique in its elimination of unnecessary walking distances for the passenger. It carries the decentralisation idea almost to its ultimate and offers great passenger convenience, for amongst other things it does not involve the need for any form of passenger transfer system. As of the moment three of the four annular terminals planned have been built. Each terminal is 2,300ft long, 65ft wide and with three levels: ramp level, passenger service level and mezzanine level (incorporating a restaurant). Each terminal car park will hold 850 cars, and 920 additional spaces are located between each terminal, for longer term parking. Provision is made for multi-level parks within the terminal circles, to provide for up to 180 spaces per gate.

On the airside each terminal has 51 aircraft gate positions. There are currently two runways with provision for more as traffic expansion dictates. In its present form the airport is capable of handling up to eight million passengers a year.

Leningrad (Shosseinaya)

USSR

Location: 9 miles south of Leningrad
Elevation: 59ft (18m)
Runways in use: 2
10/31 8,200ft × 200ft (2,500m × 60m)
10/28 11,150ft × 230ft (3,400m × 70m)

Leningrad has come to be known by an increasing number of travellers from the West and as befits the massive scope of Soviet domestic airline operations, is a large airport with an imposing passenger terminal.

Located just 370 miles to the north-west of Moscow and 1,300 miles from London, the former capital of Russia is a principal hub for the operations of Aeroflot, the state airline. Located on the 'European side' of the USSR, Leningrad is also the gateway to the West, and frequent services are operated from here to European and Scandinavian capitals.

The terminal facilities at Leningrad have undergone various stages of modernisation in the past few years, to a degree whereby the lounges are comfortable and the check-in and other facilities bear strong comparison with many other European airports. The most recent development took place in 1973, when new terminal halls were built, and a number of new facilities introduced, such as a lounge for mothers with small children. Leningrad's new terminal hall was proudly proclaimed at this date as being 'larger than a football pitch'. The terminal structure itself is of striking design, with five centrally-disposed glass towers, which give natural illumination to the cavernous hall.

Below: *Leningrad Airport offers a striking sight to the visitor, with its collection of centrally disposed glass towers, which illuminate the passenger terminal.*

Lisbon International
Portugal

Location: 4 miles from Lisbon city centre
Elevation: 374ft (114m)
Runways in use: 2
18/36 7,872ft × 150ft (2,400m × 45m)
03/21 12,480ft × 150ft (3,803m × 45m)
Airport area: 1,275 acres
Passengers handled in 1977: 2,520,000
Total aircraft movements in 1977: 46,000
Cargo handled in 1977: 41,800

From the small country of Portugal, navigators headed out across the world first with their sailing ships to colonise lands in distant parts and stamp on them the indelible Portuguese mark. In South America in the west, in India, Africa, and Timor in the east, signs of the far-ranging nature of missionaries from Imperial Portugal remain strong today, even though the country no longer has any strong overseas political power. Aviation came later, when in 1922 two Portuguese aviators, Coutinho and Cabral, made the first aerial crossing of the South Atlantic. Lisbon Airport was opened for business 20 years after that occasion, on 1 December 1942, when most of the western world was at war. For neutral Portugal this was a particularly significant occasion.

In its original form Lisbon Airport had a passenger terminal and four runways, the longest of which was 3,900ft, and which were excellent for their time. In those first years, when traffic was reduced to a shadow of what it could have been because of the

Below: *The terminal building at Lisbon International Airport, Portugal. The airport is handling 2.8 million passengers a year and some 37,000 tons of cargo.*

war, the airport nevertheless became a scheduled stopping place for almost a dozen airlines, and established Lisbon as a modern air terminal for international flights.

From the postwar period traffic steadily increased up to the point where 2.5 million passengers were being handled in 1970 and a total of 43,000 aircraft movements were being recorded annually, with consequent additions to the number of terminal facilities.

In concert with the increasing traffic, alterations have been made to the airport since the start of the jet age and up to the present time, when various plans have been drawn for a completely new airport to serve the country's capital city. The economic climate in Portugal has restrained the construction of a brand new airport, however, and for the moment developments continue at the present site.

Lisbon International is a comfortable and well-sited airport, located near the coast and just 20 minutes drive (four miles) from the city centre. The style of the terminal buildings is dated by today's standards, but the interior of the passenger halls has been steadily modernised to answer today's needs. Thirty years of operation have also been enough to establish orange and other trees which impart a friendly atmosphere at the airport.

Lisbon Airport today has two runways, the longest of which is 12,500ft, and they see 46,000 aircraft movements in total annually. The airport is served by 88 scheduled airlines and numerous non-scheduled carriers, with the bulk of this traffic being handled by the national carrier Transportes Aéreos Portugueses (TAP). In 1976 TAP was responsible for 68.3% of the passenger traffic handled at Lisbon, and accounted for 51.9% of the air transport

movements. In that year there was an average of 687 scheduled and non-scheduled commercial flights every week, with a maximum of 683 movements in one peak summer week.

Ten types of aircraft were using Lisbon Airport in 1976, with the Boeing 727 heading the list with the greatest number of movements — 40.3%. The Boeing 707 was the second busiest type at Lisbon (30%) thus illustrating a measure of the airport's noise problem, for the quieter B747 and DC-10 were at that date still only accounting for 9.3% of total movements between them. Unfortunately, Lisbon Airport creates a noise problem, which the authorities have been working hard to minimise. The number of night flights allowed has been steadily reduced, and the take-offs have been re-routed to reduce the number of movements overflying the city from 4,044 to 3,434 in 1976. This position has since improved further and will continue to improve as the noisier aircraft are phased out. Ultimately, however, a new airport for Lisbon may be the only answer to this thorny problem.

London (Heathrow)   UK

Location: 15 miles west of London
Elevation: 80ft (24m)
Runways in use: 3
10L/28R 12,792ft × 300ft (3,900m × 91m)
05R/23L 7,708ft × 300ft (2,350m × 91m)
10R/28L 11,972ft × 300ft (3,650m × 91m)
Airport area: 2,718 acres
Passengers handled in 1977: 23,775,605
Total aircraft movements in 1977: 242,998
Cargo handled in 1977: 442,100 tons

Few airports have come in for so much criticism, controversy and discussion in the press as Heathrow Airport, while at the same time handling such a large traffic and acting as a highly efficient terminal point for world-ranging airliners.

Heathrow Airport is unique in being the busiest International airport in the world, in the amount of money that is spent there annually, and in its style, which has made expanding civil air operations difficult from the outset. It is continually under fire from local residents because of the noise that it generates, and from operators because its landing fees for airliners are among the highest in the world. For the travelling public it has been called 'the world's most hated airport', while airline pilots have nothing but praise for the efficiency of the air traffic control.

Heathrow was first planned as an aerodrome in 1943 when World War II was at its height. It was clear that the Royal Air Force Transport Command would need an aerodrome for the operation of trooping flights to the Far East, and some 50 sites were examined for this purpose. The one considered to be most suitable was near Feltham in Middlesex, situated between Hounslow and Staines. There was an aerodrome already there at the time, used by the Fairey Aviation Company and known as Heathrow. This aerodrome was, in fact, not far from the original site at Hounslow Heath from where the first

Overleaf: *London Heathrow from the air, showing the limitations imposed upon expansion by the original runway design.*

Below: *Interior of Terminal 2, Heathrow.*

international civil aviation services began on 25 August 1919.

Work began on the new RAF aerodrome in 1944, but the war against Japan ended before it reached a very advanced stage, and because of its proximity to London it was subsequently decided to make this a civil airport for the capital. When it was approved that this should be the main London Airport, administration passed from the Royal Air Force to the then Ministry of Civil Aviation.

Limited operations were possible in 1946, and the first airliner to take off from the new airport was British South American Airways' Avro Lancastrian *Star Light*, which left London Airport on 1 January 1946 on a proving flight to Buenos Aires. BSAA opened a regular service on this route in March 1946. On 1 May 1946, Heathrow was officially opened to air traffic, by which time it had been named officially London Airport.

Within a few years it was clear that much work would have to be done to bring the airport up to standard if London was to have an international airport suitable for the capital, and the first of a long line of expansion programmes was begun. A new 120ft control tower was built, together with a large passenger building (now known as Terminal 2) and an administration and crew rest block, later called Queen's Building. The first of these buildings was opened for use on 17 April 1955. This area was officially named London Airport Central.

The next development scheme to be put in hand was that devised by the Millbourn Committee, which had been drawn up in the late 1950s to examine ways in which London Airport could best be expanded and utilised in the future. It was already clear that the central terminal island arrangement was confining and offered little possibility for expansion. Amongst other things, the Committee found that the best way of making the most of what they had with London Airport was to withdraw one runway from the original six planned and then withdraw a second runway from use to provide more space for building. It was also recommended that a pier system between the buildings and aprons be constructed, that a long-haul passenger terminal be erected, and that a second short-haul passenger building constructed on the north-east face.

The new long-haul passenger building, later called Terminal 3, was opened first in November 1961, at which point the original Terminal 1 was joined with the terminal used for European flights, and in this united form became known as Terminal 2. The new terminal planned to the north-east came into use in 1969, and was then designated Terminal 1. This terminal used by British Airways for domestic and European flights and subsequently by one or two European carriers, gave the airport its third passenger terminal, and this is the situation up to the present day.

Subsequent to this work the new cargo terminal, colloquially known as the Cargo Village, was built to provide air freight facilities for carriers using the airport, and which included numerous all-cargo airlines. In its initial form this terminal area covered 165 acres and cost £20 million.

On the terminal front, further work was done in the early 1970s on Terminal 3 and, adjacent to this,

a new long-haul international arrivals section was built. Air jetties were installed at the growing number of passenger piers in the central area, and the number of multi-storey car parks increased. Such developments have brought us up to the present time, when it is acknowledged that the airport is as good as saturated by passenger traffic in the peak periods of a year, and when the limit of terminal expansion has almost been reached.

Various additional measures are being taken wherever possible to provide for the ever rising tide of travellers passing through Heathrow, numbers that now make London Airport the fourth busiest in the world. Amongst these measures has been the creation of a new, £7 million terminal satellite built on the airside face of the Queen's Building, which was scheduled for completion in 1979. Built to meet the special needs of the London-Paris air bridge services established by British Airways and Air France, this terminal will offer scope for additional air bridge services to major European cities, such as Amsterdam and Brussels. It will be linked with Terminals 1 and 2 and be equipped with moving walkways.

Another recent development has been the completion of an underground rail link from Hounslow West to the centre of the airport, which makes it possible for passengers to travel from the West End of London right into the heart of the airport by the one underground train. Three years late in the construction, this underground rail link does now offer a valuable service for travellers, and compensates to some degree for the withdrawal of check-in facilities at the West London Air Terminal.

The new rail link offers no relief to the British Airport Authority providing crucially needed terminal space, however, and a fourth terminal is now a feature of the Authority's plans. To be located on the south side of the airport, Terminal 4 is intended to raise the capacity of the airport to 38 million passengers/year. This capacity is expected to be the ultimate for Heathrow, and may be reached by 1990, or before, depending upon the degree of transference of services by various airlines to Gatwick. With resistance to the move to Gatwick already hard on the part of numerous airlines, the day of officially recognised saturation may be much closer.

Top right: *Interior of Terminal 1, Heathrow.*

Right: *Composite picture of Terminal 2, illustrating new passenger channels which have been erected on the face of the terminal in the widening operation.*

Los Angeles International

USA

Location: 20 miles from Los Angeles city centre
Elevation: 126ft (38m)
Runways in use: 5
25L/07R 12,000ft × 200ft (3,657m × 60m)
25R/07L 12,090ft × 150ft (3,684m × 45m)
24L/06R 10,285ft × 150ft (3,135m × 45m)
24R/06L 8,925ft × 150ft (2,720m × 45m)
26/08 3,000ft × 75ft (914m × 23m) general
aviation; daylight hours and VFR only)
Airport area: 3,500 acres
Passengers handled in 1977: 28,361,863
Total air transport movements in 1977: 431,811
Cargo handled in 1977: 812,283 tons

Apart from being the third busiest airport in the world, both in terms of passenger traffic handled and aircraft movements, LAX as the airport is otherwise known, is noteworthy in being based on the satellite concept of design, in which individual passenger terminals are reached by tunnels from the central area. This involved the placing around the central section of satellite buildings served directly by the aircraft taxying in from the adjoining pairs of parallel runways. The sytem thus decentralises traffic while

Below: *The Court of Flags fronts the 172ft high control tower and administration block at Los Angeles International Airport, third busiest in the world.*

at the same time gives as much freedom to aircraft as possible, and eliminates congestion of the central area. This is given over to car parks (there is space for a total of 18,000 cars), the main restaurants and the airport's control tower and administration building.

In 1926 the city of Los Angeles first considered establishing a municipal airport near Inglewood and in 1927 a group of local citizens chose 640 acres of a ranch area for the airport site. In 1928 one Clifford Henderson was appointed the first director of the 'airport', which in fact, comprised a dirt strip for the runway and no buildings, and was called Mines Field. In the same year the city of Los Angeles leased the present site of the airport for 50 years for a rent of $124,800 a year. Two 100ft hangars were built on the south side of the airport at a cost of $35,000 each. On 7 June 1930 the airport was officially opened, and in 1932 the famous Douglas Aircraft Company began operations at the airport. Four years later Douglas was joined by the North American Aviation company, which erected a plant at the airport with 90,000sq ft of floor space.

The postwar years saw the big development of the airport, and in 1949 the airport was officially renamed Los Angeles International. In December 1957 ground-breaking was begun for the start of a jet age terminal and other improvements, the terminal being dedicated by the then vice president,

Lyndon B. Johnson. In June 1962, with the dedication of the International Carriers Satellite, the new jet age terminal complex became fully operational.

The $100 million terminal at LAX was built under the administration of the Board of Airport Commissioners and the Los Angeles Department of Airports, and occupies 265 acres of the 3,500-acre airport site. The terminal is made up of the individual-ticketing and satellite units, which are constructed on two levels. There are 13 ticketing-satellite buildings, which are two storeys high with provision for a third storey when required. The first floor, on the parking level, is given over to ticketing and baggage facilities. The second floor is for administrative use. The ticketing buildings are connected to their individual satellites by underground channels, some 400ft long and 20ft wide, which enable passengers to reach the aircraft manoeuvring areas without being in the way of the aircraft and many vehicles operating on the surface. This routing also directs passengers to particular parts of the airport for specific flights. Each satellite, built on the apron level, is able to service 12 jet aircraft simultaneously. With most airlines at LAX passengers board the aircraft by way of airbridges, which means the passengers never usually set foot on the apron. The satellite terminals contain lobby areas, restaurants, news-stands and other public rooms.

The two northerly terminals, which adjoin parallel runways 06L and 06R, are used by international carriers, while the satellite terminals to the south are used by US carriers. To the west of the central area

Above: The dramatic sprawl of Los Angeles International shows here the centrally disposed Theme Building, with its 300-seat restaurant placed under the lofty parabolic arches, on the left, and one of the two international carrier satellite terminals in the foreground. The US airline terminals are at the rear. The car parks hold up to 18,000 cars.

is a commuter terminal, used by air taxi aircraft and commercial helicopters as well as third-level operators.

Los Angeles International runs down to the Pacific Ocean, and is separated from the sea by only a small housing estate and the Vista Del Mar, a seafront drive. Overlooking the airports and the twin pairs of runways, is the 172ft high control tower building. Next to this impressive building is the Theme Building, which is in fact a restaurant building constructed in parabolic arches which soar 135ft above the ground. The airport authorities say that this Theme Building symbolises the futuristic character of the airport, and they have placed the restaurant among the arches 70ft above the ground; it will accommodate 300 diners, who have an all round view of the airport's activities from this lofty perch.

With its first 50 years of operation behind it, Los Angeles International is considering the possibility of 40 million passengers a year using the airport by 1984. Further developments, such as improving access roads and additional terminal improvements, will be required, and plans are already being studied to this end.

Manchester (Ringway)

Location: 7.5 miles SSW of Manchester
Elevation: 256ft (75m)
Runways in use: 2
06/24 9,200ft × 150ft (2,800m × 45m)
10/28 2,950ft × 150ft (900m × 45m) (general aviation)
Airport area: 1,342 acres
Passengers handled in 1977: 2,903,968
Total aircraft movements in 1977: 59,535
Cargo handled in 1977: 37,468 tons

The first site for Manchester Airport was at Wythenshawe, selected in 1929. Within a year, however, this site was replaced by an airport at Barton in 1930, and some £51,000 was spent on the development of that airport. The Barton site remained Manchester's airport until the search began in 1934 for a better location. This was found at Ringway, just a few miles from Wythenshawe, and on 25 June 1938 Manchester (Ringway) Airport was opened officially by HM Secretary of State for Air, Sir Kingsley Wood.

The first aircraft to use the airport was a Douglas DC-2 belonging to KLM, which actually flew into Ringway on 24 June 1938. The airport at that time consisted largely of a prepared grass landing area, and covered some 250 acres. Subsequently Manchester Corporation purchased a total of 660 acres to permit further development. Additional ground has been purchased since to bring the airport to its present size. The airport was impressed into service for the RAF when the war came, and the first runways were laid.

Postwar operation of the airport was finally vested in Manchester Corporation in 1953, when the Corporation settled with the Ministry of Aviation the airport's ownership and management. Five years later Manchester Corporation embarked on a large

Below: Manchester Airport's fine control tower and terminal block. The airport is used by an increasing number of international carriers on scheduled services.

scale improvement plan for the airport, a prime feature of which was a fine new control tower and terminal building. This was opened by HRH the Duke of Edinburgh on 22 October 1962.

Another feature of this development scheme was the creation of two piers, one for domestic and one for international flights, the longer of which stretched for 970ft across the apron. By 1968 the airport was handling two million passengers/year. Another feature was the installation of a hydrant fuel system, which eliminated the need for large numbers of tankers moving about the apron to refuel aircraft.

In 1973 further development work was put in hand to fit the airport for Jumbo jets and to raise its capacity to five million passengers annually by 1982. This programme involved the doubling of the capacity of the control tower administration block for operational purposes; the erection of an additional long-haul pier, to be equipped with airbridges, the construction of a 13-level carpark, the enlargement of the international departure and transit lounge, the provision of a new Immigration and Customs hall, and the extension of the whole southern airside frontage at first and second floor levels. A number of other works were included.

The new pier can accept in the nose-in position four wide-bodied aircraft and one narrow, or seven B707 types. The original international pier is regularly occupied by 14 large aircraft. At the moment the airport is handling three million passengers a year.

Manchester has a problem as an international airport in that it has a single 9,200ft long runway for transport aircraft, and a second runway has been desired since 1973. Approval for construction of this second main runway was received in 1975, but subsequently various authorities and objecting parties delayed its actual construction. The passage of time coupled with hesitancy on the part of Manchester Airport Authority itself has seen the cost of this construction task escalate from £8 million to almost £30 million in 1978. At the time of publication it is uncertain whether this second runway will be constructed in the early future.

Melbourne (Tullamarine) Australia

Location: 12 miles NW of Melbourne
Elevation: 354ft (108m)
Runways in use: 2
16/34 12,005ft x 150ft (3,660m x 45m)
09/27 7,500ft x 150ft (2,287m x 45m)
Airport area: 5,300 acres
Passengers handled in 1977: 5,048,847
Total aircraft movements in 1977: 89,885
Cargo handled in 1977: 80,515 tons

Above: Melbourne's Tullamarine Airport was built to replace a former airport at Essendon. The airport is built on a plateau, 400ft above sea level.

The provision of major international air terminals on the great continent of Australia is paramount to a country which is the biggest island in the world. Sydney and Melbourne have both had airports since 1921, with the present Sydney Airport located in substantially the same place, nine miles from the city centre, as when it began services to civil aviation. Melbourne Airport has had several locations however, varying in the last 58 years from 4-12 miles from the city centre.

In 1958 the Australian Department of Civil Aviation convened a panel to consider the possibilities of a future airport for Melbourne. After due deliberation, the panel recommended the development of the Tullamarine area, while at the same time pronouncing that no further extension could be made to the existing airport, at Essendon. Examination of the airspace requirements for the area finally determined that Tullamarine should be the site developed, and Australian Government approval was obtained in 1959 to acquire the necessary 5,300 acres of land required for the planned airport.

The airport was introduced into service on a phased basis from 1970, when terminal facilities for international operations were completed first. Domestic terminal facilities were introduced gradually from 1971, and the transfer of major operators from Essendon to the new Melbourne Airport was made from that time.

Situated on an area of gently sloping land almost 400ft above sea level, Melbourne Tullamarine is bounded to the east and west by deep valleys. The soil is a clay type, but drainage conditions are excellent. There is ample space for future expansion, and duplication of the runway system if necessary. A freeway was constructed by the State Roads Authority, and links the airport and its approaches to the centre of Melbourne. An internal road system connects various areas of the airport with each other and to the external roads. An elevated roadway runs along the face of the terminal building at first floor level, and provides access to the terminal for departing passengers arriving by airport bus or taxi. There is a seven-acre landscaped car park fronting the terminal building accommodating 1,200 cars. With other car parks, to the north, south and east, there is room in the terminal area for over 5,000 cars.

The terminal complex design comprises an angular terminal with three sections, the central section being the longest. Facing a wide apron, each of the three terminal sections is equipped with a pier, or loading concourse. The central pier is an enclosed structure of two storeys, 570ft long and terminating in a Y with two stub piers at its end. This constitutes the international loading concourse. The north and south concourses, stretching as straight piers across the apron, are used primarily for domestic operations, depending upon traffic flow at Melbourne. The design is straightforward and uncluttered, and accommodates all the usual facilities required for the handling and clearance of arriving and departing passengers. At each aircraft parking position there is a holding lounge for passengers, who board their aircraft by way of airbridges from the upper level of the two storeys in each pier; the apron level is given over to mechanical services, baggage handling and airline duties.

An initial two runways were laid down, and the pavements of these constructed to accept aircraft of up to 800,000lb weight. The runways are to standard ICAO specification as to width, that is 150ft with 25ft paved shoulders, and are generally flexible, with 58in to 64in thicknesses. Because the runways were built virtually parallel to those at the Essendon Airport, they are operated within the same air traffic control pattern. The runways incorporate high speed turnoffs, which enable aircraft to leave the runways at speeds of up to 60mph, and which as a result clears the runways more swiftly for following aircraft, thereby increasing the airport's handling capacity, particularly at peak periods.

Melbourne Tullamarine is now handling over five million passengers a year, and is expected to see the Concorde among its visiting aircraft before long.

Milan (Malpensa/Linate) Italy

MALPENSA

Location: 30 miles NW of Milan in the Province of Varese
Elevation: 767ft (234m)
Runways in use: 2
17L/35R 12,844ft x 200ft (3,915m x 60m)
17R/35L 8,620ft x 200ft (2,628m x 60m)
Passengers handled in 1977: 1,229,952
Total aircraft movements in 1977: 14,254
Cargo handled in 1977: 41,075 tons

LINATE

Location: 4 miles east of Milan
Elevation: 352ft (108m)
Runways in use: 2
18/36 7,337ft x 200ft (2,236m x 60m)
1,968ft x 72ft (600m x 22m) (general aviation)
Passengers handled in 1977: 5,103,263
Total aircraft movements in 1977: 79,414
Cargo handled in 1977: 60,380 tons

Milan has two airports, Malpensa and Linate, of which Linate is the older in terms of international air traffic, but Malpensa is the larger and the one earmarked for future development as Milan's principal airport.

Both airports have a history which dates back to the early 1900s, for the Italian aeronautical engineer Gianni Caproni established a base at Linate for his aircraft work in about 1930, while the famous Italian designer Giovanni Agusta had associations with Malpensa from as early as 1907. In 1924 an airport was built at Malpensa, and used by the military in later years, and at Linate the first civil airport was built in 1930, when the site was named Aeroporto Enrico Forlanini, in memory of the Italian aeronautical pioneer.

Both airports were used after the war for commercial traffic and Malpensa was turned into an airport for larger aircraft in November 1948 when modernisation was begun. Linate underwent a similar facelift in 1958-62. By now, however, a new airport service company, created for the development and management of both airports had been brought into being, and this company, Societa Esercizi Aeroportuali, otherwise known as SEA, was created as an autonomous association with 84.5% of the share capital held by the Milan Municipality and 14.5% by Milan Province.

SEA decreed that both airports be modernised and that Linate be assigned to domestic traffic only, with Malpensa becoming the intercontinental airport. In 1972 the Italian Ministry of Transport approved a new master plan for Malpensa which will extend its traffic handling capability up to the year 2000. Milan-Malpensa is the airport on which prime work is being concentrated. The master plan provides for a passenger terminal with a potential for handling up to 12 million passengers a year, at a throughflow rate of 7,500 passengers an hour. The building will have seven floors and a depth towards the apron of about 300ft. There will be two satellites, and parking space on the air side for about 20 aircraft in the nose-in position. These aircraft will be reached by air bridges. Other aircraft, parked in remoter positions, will be served by apron buses.

The master plan for development of Malpensa provides also for a new air freight terminal, a bonded warehouse, Customs building, buildings for airline operators, airport personnel and large car parks.

Below: Landside view of Milan-Malpensa Airport, which is being developed according to a new master plan for traffic up to the year 2000.

Bottom: Milan-Malpensa will be equipped with airbridges in due course.

Moscow (Vnukovo/Sheremetievo)

VNUKOVO

Location: 17 miles SW of Moscow
Elevation: 669ft (204m)
Runways in use: 2
02/20 10,000ft × 200ft (3,050m × 60m)
06/24 9,840ft × 260ft (3,000m × 80m)

SHEREMETIEVO

Location: 17 miles NNW of Moscow
Elevation: 623ft (190m)
Runways in use: 1
07/25 11,480ft × 260ft (3,500m × 80m)
Passengers handled in 1976: 3,949,000
Total aircraft movements in 1976: 67,900
Cargo handled in 1976: 60,000 tons

Moscow has four principal airports, Vnukovo, Sheremetievo, Bykovo and Domodedovo, of which Vnukovo was originally the main one. This was superseded by Sheremetievo in 1960 as the new major international airport for the capital, however, and Vnukovo has been relegated to handling shorter, domestic passenger flights. Of the others, Bykovo has been in existence for some years now and serves principally as cargo airport for the capital. The fourth of the quartet, Domodedovo, was opened for international passenger operations in 1966.

Vnukovo dates from pre-World War II days, when it had only a grass operational strip and a small terminal building. In postwar years it became the

Below: Domodedovo Airport, Moscow, one of the principal airports of the four currently serving the Soviet capital.

usual arrival airport for heads of state visiting the Soviet capital. A second airport terminal was constructed near the original one at Vnukovo, able to handle some 2,000 passengers an hour. While the airport has now given way to Sheremetievo as the international air gateway, it is still regarded as important to the Moscow airport system.

Domodedovo is one of the biggest airports in Europe, and while no information is available on the matter, it is almost certain that flights have been made to the airport by the Tupolev Tu-144 supersonic airliner since that airliner began scheduled flights from Moscow to Alma Ata in 1977.

The airport terminal building is 350yd long, interconnected with a control office, which oversees ramp services. The waiting hall covers a floor area of over 32,000sq ft. There is a balcony and roof garden in the building. On the outside, there are western style passenger piers, while on the landside there is parking space for over 1,000 cars.

Moscow's prime international airport, Sheremetievo, has certainly been seeing flights by the Tu-144 as well as all of the biggest and heaviest jets in international service. Sheremetievo is a good-looking airport, with no dramatic frills, but with spacious and well-lit terminal buildings, and the overall premises have a volume of some 5.3 million cubic feet. The terminals have been handling traffic throughputs of 2,000 passengers an hour. The airport is served by electric railway trains as well as bus services; there is also a heliport. The facilities at Sheremetievo are currently being expanded in preparation for the 1980 Moscow Olympics. The Moscow Olympics are serving partly as an occasion for the opportunity to further modernise the airport, however, and this is considered as only one move in a plan to further expand Moscow's airport system.

The other and principal move is the construction of a brand new airport, located 37 miles north-west of the centre of the capital and called Sheremetievo II. This new airport, otherwise known as Olympic Airport, is scheduled to be completed and handed over to the Soviet authorities in December 1979, or some months before the start of the 22nd Olympic Games.

Olympic Airport is being built by the German company Rüterbau of Hanover, a subsidiary of the Salzgitter organisation, which won the contract for the project in May 1977 in competition with 30 well-known companies from all over the world. It will cost some DM230 million and Rüterbau will have a participating stake in the project of some DM 35 million. The company was responsible for the recently-built replacement passenger terminal for Hanover Airport, and to which the Olympic Airport terminal bears a striking resemblance.

The design of Sheremetievo II Airport has been based upon four prime requirements. It must be able to handle up to 2,100 passengers an hour in the peak period; to handle six million passengers a year; to serve simultaneously 19 aircraft of different types,

and to cover no more than 915,000sq ft in terminal area. Negotiation of the contract between Rüterbau and the Soviet authorities occupied 18 months. With all requirements met, construction work began in July 1977. This construction work is being done largely by German technicians and personnel, with prefabricated building sections being transported to Moscow from the Federal Republic of Germany.

The airport of Sheremetievo II is to be used exclusively for international flights, and should be a showcase in the Moscow airport system. There will be two terminals integrated with a central administrative building, and two pairs of parallel runways.

Below: Apron at Sheremetievo Airport, Moscow, with a line of Tu-104s joined by a Caravelle of Air France and a British Airways B707.

Bottom: The new airport of Sheremetievo II, or Olympia Airport, has been designed to handle six million passengers a year. It is being constructed by the West German firm Rüterbau, and is scheduled to be in service for the Moscow Olympic Games in 1980.

Newcastle (Woolsington)

UK

Location: 5.5 miles NW of Newcastle
Elevation: 266ft (80m)
Runways in use: 1
07/25 7,672ft × 150ft (2,339m × 45m)
Passengers handled in 1977: 741,802
Total aircraft movements in 1977: 25,453
Cargo handled in 1977: 4,694 tons

Since 1967 Newcastle Airport has had a terminal building and pier complex which make it one of the best-looking airports in the north-east of England. Probably more importantly, this terminal complex has transformed Newcastle from the small regional airport that it was, into one capable of handling the biggest jets and an annual traffic of almost 1,000,000 passengers a year, at a rate of 650 passengers an hour. The airport is now handling ten operators, including Pan American, TWA, Britannia Airways and Dan-Air, on a regular basis, and expects to attract more, including all-cargo operators.

The airport was first opened on 26 July 1935 by the then Secretary of State for Air, Sir Philip Cunliffe-Lister. A first 345 acres of land was bought for the Municipal Airport, and modest services began that year. Operations were short-lived, for the airport was taken over for war service in 1939, and it was not until the postwar period, when the airport was de-requisitioned and handed back to the local authority, that air transport services were able to grow.

In April 1963 a North-East Regional Airport Committee was formed, and this included representatives of the County Councils of Durham and Northumberland, Newcastle-upon-Tyne and the County Boroughs of Gateshead, South Shields, Tynemouth and Sunderland. This committee took over responsibility for the operation and development of the airport, and a first action was to appoint the British company of Sir Frederick Snow & Partners as consulting engineers to advise on development of the airport. The firm's report was submitted in July 1963 and provided for staged development of the airport to equip it for meeting the growing air transport demands in the region. Construction work began on the runway and a new control building in November 1964 and these were opened for use in April 1966. The new terminal complex, complete with passenger finger, was officially opened on 17 February 1967, by the then Prime Minister, the Rt Hon Harold Wilson.

The airport today is a good-looking facility with a terminal built on a reinforced concrete frame and finished with a covering of white ceramic tiles. To achieve ease of passenger flow, the forecourt is at concourse level, which is the first floor of the building. On the airside at ground level a pier extends across the apron to provide cover for the passengers between the terminal and the aircraft. There is an airport restaurant, a large buffet lounge, cocktail bar and viewing gallery as well as the usual facilities of shops, telephones, car hire and postal and information services.

For the future the master plan provides for further development of the terminal building, extension of the runway and provision for Category II ILS, construction of a cargo building, and further expansion of the car parks to provide for spaces additional to the present 1,000, probably in a covered, multi-storey facility. The airport already has an hotel, which was opened in March 1973.

Below: Newcastle has had an airport since 1935, but the present terminal complex was opened in 1967.

Location: 15 miles SE of Manhattan, New York
Elevation: 12ft (3.6m)
Runways in use: 5
04R/22L 8,400ft x 150ft (2,560m x 45m)
04L/22R 11,352ft x 150ft (3,460m x 45m)
13L/31R 10,000ft x 150ft (3,048m x 45m)
13R/31L 14,572ft x 150ft (4,440m x 45m)
14/32 2,760ft x 75ft (1,054m x 23m) (general aviation)
Airport area: 4,930 acres
Passengers handled in 1977: 22,545,497
Total air transport movements in 1977: 294,100
Cargo handled in 1977: 1,191,035 tons

New York International Airport, known since December 1963 as John F. Kennedy, is another of the world's airports which has been built largely on tracts of land reclaimed from the sea. The airport was first planned in 1942, and its site was originally occupied by a golf course and the waters of Jamaica Bay, off New York City. The city filled in this site at a cost of $60 million and leased it to the Port Authority of New York and New Jersey. This lease has run since June 1947, and saw the original dedication of the airport on 31 July 1948. Commercial flights from the airport actually began on 1 July 1948.

Above: Kennedy International, distinctive for its individual airline terminals built round the central area.
Overleaf: United Airlines' passenger terminal at JFK International, with articulated airbridges in use.

Initially, an airport of 1,100 acres was planned, or one about twice the size of La Guardia, which was becoming inadequate for both international and domestic traffic. It was not envisaged that the airport would eventually be nine times the size of La Guardia and cover 4,930 acres, or an area equivalent to all of Manhattan Island from 42nd Street to the Battery, at the southern end of the Island.

In 1952 the PNYA completed an 11-storey control tower, built 11 hangars and an air route traffic control centre. In March 1955 construction work began on a new central area of the airport called Terminal City which covered 655 acres Features of this airport city were the international Arrivals Building and two adjacent foreign flag wing buildings, individual terminal buildings for US airlines, a central heating and refrigeration plant, five car parks, a 220-acre, landscaped international park, 7.5 miles of taxiways and 10 miles of two-lane roads. The official dedication of the first part of

Above: *Newark Airport, third of New York's main passenger airports, employs the radial satellite system of terminal buildings, connected to the main terminals by two-storey piers. Newark is becoming a major charter flight airport.*

Terminal City took place on 5 December 1957, and the Arrivals Building was opened on 6 December 1957.

Today, the central area consists of nine passenger terminals surrounded by a dual ring of aircraft taxiways. Originally 655 acres, this area was enlarged to 840 acres. There is provision in the central area for 6,600 cars, while in total there are 13,000 public car parking places at the airport. Amongst the many facilities for travellers there is an international hotel with 520 rooms, three car rental buildings, a bus garage, and numerous shops, observation decks and restaurants. The airport is now handling almost 23 million passengers a year and employs 41,000 people. To date the Port Authority has invested some $673 million in the airport.

A feature of John F. Kennedy International is the arrangement whereby various airlines have erected and operate their own passenger terminals, and thus US flag carriers Pan American, Trans World Airlines, Eastern Air Lines, United Airlines, American Airlines and Northwest Airlines have their own individually styled terminals, dramatic in design and efficient in function. There is also a joint British Airways/Air

Canada terminal, while Lufthansa and Air France also have terminal facilities of their own. At present there are 145 aircraft gate positions serving the various terminals. There are 13 US scheduled airlines serving the airport, including the helicopter operator New York Airways, 16 US and foreign charter airlines and 45 overseas airlines, making 74 airlines in total.

Air cargo has become so substantial at JFK that the airport has developed into one of the most important air cargo centres in the world, and indeed is currently handling the greatest cargo tonnage amongst all of the world's airports. In 1977 this was 1,191,03 tons, which was 16% more than in 1976. With 45 foreign airlines and 12 US cargo-carrying airlines using the airport, it became necessary to provide a special air cargo centre at JFK, and which is the largest in the United States. This occupies 344 acres and includes 22 cargo buildings, providing 2.5 million square feet. Not suprisingly, perhaps, with such a vast cargo throughout, large-scale theft problems were experienced at one stage. There are now 35 airfreight forwarders, Customs brokers and consolidator companies on the airport was well as numerous trucking firms and several Federal agencies.

There are two pairs of parallel runways at JFK while a fifth runway serves general aviation, private and business flying. The whole complex is overseen by the 150ft high control tower, which houses $1 million worth of air traffic control electronic equipment.

New York (La Guardia)

USA

Location: 8 miles from Manhattan, New York
Elevation: 21ft (6m)
Runways in use: 3
04/22 7,000ft × 150ft (2,133m × 45m)
13/31 7,000ft × 150ft (2,133m × 45m)
14/32 2,000ft × 75ft (610m × 23m)
Airport area: 650 acres
Passengers handled in 1977: 15,087,530
Total air transport movements in 1977: 238,900
Cargo handled in 1977: 48,936 tons

Known until the ascendancy of Kennedy International as 'New York's own', La Guardia Airport is named after the one-time mayor of New York City who was primarily instrumental in gaining its development as an airport to serve the business capital of the USA. Fiorello La Guardia achieved his ambition of securing the airport for New York City in September 1937. Before that the one-time amusement park site had been used as a private flying field from 1929, when it was first named Glenn H. Curtiss Airport, and then North Beach Airport.

The airport was opened to commercial traffic on 2 December 1939 when the original site, covering 105 acres, was enlarged by the City's filling in the waterfront on the airport's east side. The airport grew into a 558-acre tract and then to cover 630 acres. It has been enlarged further in the last decade, and now covers 650 acres overall. It grew also to have three active runways and a large and elegant terminal complex fronted by a car park which was once a boat basin.

Today, New York's own airport continues to handle 15 million passengers/year and employ almost 9,000 people.

Operated by the Port Authority of New York and New Jersey, La Guardia plays a central role in the New York airport system as a largely domestic airport channelling passengers between New York City and the nation's west and south. In this task it is an important complementary airport to John F. Kennedy, which airport is now the principal hub for New York.

An expansion programme for the airport was begun in 1958, and then in 1964 a new central passenger terminal was completed, costing $36 million. This was nearly seven times larger than the original 1939 terminal and provides 650,000sq ft of floor space. It consists of a four storey central section, two three-storey wings and four bi-level arcades leading to 36 aircraft gates. The first and second floor lobbies of the central section of the building have retail shops and consumer services,

Below: *La Guardia Airport, New York, was built for the days of flying-boats, but is now served by wide-bodied jets, including the A300 Airbus. The central structure behind main terminal is a multi-storey car park, erected in 1976.*

Above: *Main terminal building at La Guardia Airport, New York, on the East River side of the city, eight miles from Manhattan.*

which include a hairdresser's, post office, bookstall, hobby shop and a drugstore. There is a completely equipped nursery, a conference centre and the La Guardia Terrace Restaurant.

Under the development scheme completed in 1964 the oval car park in front of the terminal building provided for parked cars on a single lower level. The pressures of space at the airport required that this car park be enlarged, however, and the one way this could be done was by constructing a multi-level structure on the site, and this was completed at the end of 1976, at a cost of $30 million, or slightly less than the cost of the complete terminal in 1964. The new car park houses 2,900 cars adjacent to the terminal; in total there are spaces for 6,000 cars at the airport.

La Guardia is also an important air cargo facility for US airlines, and air cargo warehouses at the airport provide 35,000sq ft of space. Cargo traffic at the airport has been in decline since 1973, when almost 62,000 tons were handled, but 49,000 tons were still shifted in 1977.

A further important development became the subject of discussion at La Guardia in 1978, when one of the airport's prime users, Eastern Air Lines, contracted to buy 23 A300 Airbuses from Airbus Industrie of Toulouse. Buying these aircraft for its New York-Miami service, Eastern was presented with the problem of the aircraft being 8,000lb heavier in take-off weight than the airport's runway extensions could support. The airport was built originally in an era of flying-boats, and the runway extensions were constructed in 1967, and built on piers extending across the water in Flushing Bay. With the order of the European Airbuses by Eastern as positive, the Port Authority agreed to strengthen these runway extensions, at a cost of an estimated $850,000.

Nice (Côte d'Azur)   France

Location: 3.5 miles SW of Nice
Elevation: 12ft (3.7m)
Runways in use: 1
05/23 9,840ft × 200ft (3,000m × 60m)
Passengers handled in 1977: 2,837,923
Total aircraft movements in 1977: 59,865
Cargo handled in 1977: 10,988 tons

Above: The water-based airport of Nice Cote d'Azur is being developed according to a grand plan for the whole region, which will eventually provide for a marine harbour created to the south of the runways, built on to the whole artificial land mass.

Aviation history owes as much to Europe as it does to the USA, and some of Europe's earliest flying was done near the spot where a fine international airport stands today. It is known for example, that French pioneer aviator Captain Louis Ferber made flights with Lilienthal-type gliders at Nice, and in 1910, when aviation was well and truly launched, the town of Nice organised a grand aerial meeting for European aviators, at which prizes of up to Fr215,000 were offered, and at which records for both speed and altitude were established on aeroplanes like the Antoinette.

Then in 1920 the actual site of today's airport adopted the name of the California airfield because of the flying that was taking place there, and a 700m long grass runway was laid down. Sporting flying intensified at the airfield between 1922 and 1933. In 1936 the French company Potez Aéro-Service began a service between Nice and Toulouse and Bordeaux. The war interrupted continuance of this service.

The invasion of France by the Allies in 1944 saw the construction of a hard runway over 4,000ft long, and when the war finished in 1945 Air France installed an airline office with a view to commercial services. By 1949 the runway had been strengthened and lengthened to almost 6,000ft and air services were operating from Nice to London, Geneva, Tehran, Brazzaville and even Saigon. In 1955 the site was officially confirmed as that for the regional airport, and the airport was accorded the name Nice-Cote d'Azur.

By 1957 600,000 passengers a year were flying from Nice and it now looked very different from the sporting airfield of Captain Ferber's days and the enthusiasts of the California airfield. Nice-Cote d'Azur now sported an attractive little terminal, a cargo warehouse and well laid out car parks. By 1969, 12 years later, this terminal had been extended to accommodate travellers from the jet age, now spilling out of Air France's Caravelles and Boeing 707s, and the modest freight warehouse now stretched to long freight sheds equipped with mechanised handling devices. The car parks were becoming crowded for, as the hub of the French Riveria, Nice was now also the principal point of entry for tourists flying in from all parts of the globe. Indeed, 'the blue coast' is fittingly named for tourist purposes, and the expansion of Nice airport and tourism in the region have gone hand-in-hand.

The single runway at the airport was further lengthened and improved and by 1973 stretched to 9,840ft (3,000m). The limits of its possible extension were being reached however, for Nice is a water-based airport, with its terminal right on the coast overlooking the Baie des Anges, and with its original runway built on a strip of land literally within a few metres of the water. This beautiful location appeared to limit prospects for future development for big jets, but as airport planners have increasingly come to know, water can be as much of a friend to the landplane as it was to the flying-boat. In a dramatic decision in 1973 the French Secretary-General for Civil Aviation agreed in principle with the Nice Airport planners that a new runway could be added to the site, adjacent to the first, and built on land reclaimed from the sea and augmented by artificial filling. The runway capacity would therefore be completely doubled with this advanced plan and the prospect opened up for an eventual handling of 10 million passengers a year. In 1977 Nice handled 2,837,923 passengers in total.

The second runway was just one prime feature of a far-reaching airport development plan, which will see a complete redevelopment and modernisation of the whole airport, and which accords with a development plan for the Nice region. Amongst other things a future Port de Commerce is planned, with a harbour for ships incorporated in the land mass being developed to the south of the present and future runways, and which will thereby link land, sea and air facilities in one massive and remarkable complex.

In its present form Nice-Cote d'Azur is handling 2.3 million arriving and departing passengers annually (excluding transit, and others), and seeing almost 60,000 movements a year. Additionally, 11,000 tons of freight and 7,000 tons of mail are handled from what is essentially a holiday airport. This is perhaps a good example of how leisure can become big business.

Oslo (Fornebu)   Norway

Location: 5 miles from Oslo
Elevation: 52ft (16m)
Runways in use: 2
06/24 7,216ft × 165ft (2,200m × 50m)
01/19 5,740ft × 165ft (1,750m × 50m)
(Seaplane port also available)
Passengers handled in 1977: 2,763,000
Total aircraft movements in 1977: 52,520
Cargo handled in 1977: 24,170 tonnes

As with many Scandinavian airports, the capital city airport of Norway is under pressure because of the growth of traffic and because the geography of

Below: Fornebu Airport, Oslo, is now giving problems to the authorities and to airlines in that it is size-limited and offers no possibilities for further expansion. It is bounded by the sea on three sides.

Norway places limits upon expansion of present sites.

An attractively situated airport, Oslo's Fornebu was planned and built by the city of Oslo and opened for traffic in June 1939. It is located about five miles from the heart of Oslo and surrounded by the sea on three sides.

The prewar life of the airport was brief, and during World War II the airport was used by the Germans for military purposes. It reopened for civil operations in February 1946, and since Junce 1947 has been owned and operated by the Norwegian Government,

through the Civil Aviation Administration. It has been gradually enlarged, and a new passenger terminal was opened in 1964. This terminal has 10 aircraft gate positions.

The airport is served by 12 international and domestic airlines, and in 1977 almost 2.8 million passengers used the airport. A development plan to increase the potential of Fornebu was submitted to the Norwegian Government in 1977, and the conclusions over this have still to be presented. If a new airport for Oslo is built it may be at Hobö, about 19 miles to the south of Oslo.

Paris (Orly/Charles de Gaulle)   France

ORLY
Location: 9 miles south of Paris
Elevation: 292ft (89m)
Runways in use: 4
07/25 11,972ft × 150ft (3,650m × 45m)
08/26 10,990ft × 150ft (3,320m × 45m)
02/20 7,870ft × 200ft (2,400m × 60m)
20/02 6,110ft × 200ft (1,865m × 60m)
Airport area: 3,750 acres
Passengers handled in 1977: 12,557,316
Total aircraft movements in 1977: 161,900
Cargo handled in 1977: 163,000 tons

CHARLES DE GAULLE
Location: 12 miles from Notre Dame, Paris
Elevation: 295ft (90m)
Runways in use:1
11,800ft × 150ft (3,600m × 45m)
Airport area: 7,400 acres
Passengers handled in 1977: 8,605,297
Total aircraft movements in 1977: 86,900
Cargo handled in 1977: 284,000 tons

It can be said fairly that the airports of Paris have always been important and they have always generally been magnificent too. From the time of the commencement of air transport services in 1919, Le

Bourget played a part, after its initial start as a military grass airfield, and it went on to see the arrival of Charles Lindbergh on his solo transatlantic flight of May 1927 and then service as the principal airport for Paris right up to the time of the Jumbo jet age.

Even now Le Bourget functions, as a light aviation aerodrome and the site of the biennial Paris Air Show (Salon de l'Aéronautique et de l'Espace), while Orly Airport, to the south of the city, has taken on the role of secondary airport to the French capital and one at which a massive volume of traffic is handled annually. Orly, in fact, was assuming greater importance even as the decision was taken to replace Le Bourget, and if its position today as the second airport for Paris appears misplaced, it is simply because the grand new facility of Charles de Gaulle Airport was planned right from the outset to become the major international hub for the French capital.

As of the moment, however, Orly Airport is by no means taking a back seat, for it is handling more

Below: *Terminal building at Orly-Sud, seen from the approach road.*

traffic than CDG, and will doubtless continue to handle a heavy traffic until its facilities have to give way to the more expansive and far superior arrangements at the bigger new airport.

Orly was created on a plateau to the south of Paris and some six miles from the Porte d'Italie. It originally consisted of 629 acres of grassland, and in 1939 was made into a flying school for French Navy pilots. It was taken over by the Germans during the war, and in the first postwar year of 1946 was thought by the French Government to have potential for a future civil aerodrome. In 1949 this thinking was turned into a plan for action, and in 1954 basic studies were made for new works. These were initiated in 1957.

The new terminal buildings at Orly were opened in February 1961 by the President of the French Republic, General de Gaulle, who, as it happened, was to have his own airport memorial 13 years later in the form of the new airport at Roissy-en-France, just six miles north-east of Le Bourget.

The terminal structures today constitute two principal buildings, Orly-Sud and Orly-Ouest. Orly-Sud is a straight forward box-like structure straddling the main autoroute to the south, Route National No 7, and within this terminal are the usual multiplicity of passenger services, including an excellent hotel. The building has its own control tower for aircraft operations at the western end, and there are two piers with satellite holding lounges at either end, to the west and to the east.

Orly-Ouest is a much larger facility at the Orly site, with two extended pier terminals stretching from the main building and which between them provide parking stands for a dozen large aircraft, served by passenger bridges. This is the more recent development at Orly, and together with the Orly-Sud facility the whole complex combines to create an international airport which ranks among the busiest in Europe. In 1977 Orly Airport handled well over 12 million passengers.

The later development in the Paris airport system has been Roissy, otherwise Charles de Gaulle Airport, which was opened for service on 13 March

1974. In looking for a site for this airport the planners of the Aeroport de Paris (Paris Airport Authority) were distinctly fortunate, for when they began research in 1957 it proved there was a region known as the Plain of Old France no more than 20km (12 miles) from Notre Dame, with land occupied by very few buildings. In the event, just one farm had to be demolished when construction work began in 1966, and even here a wood was left intact as it was skirted by the terminal roads. It is the PAA's intention ultimately to plant up to 50,000 trees on the site as part of a planned beautification programme to blend the airport into the landscape.

The location of the airport is near to the place known as Roissy-en-France, and for this reason it was originally called Roissy Airport, or otherwise Paris Nord. It was given the name Charles de Gaulle Airport in early 1974 at the time of the official opening.

In every sense this new Paris airport is grand and impressive. For a start the whole site covers 7,400 acres, which, while not occupied at the present, will doubtless be taken up by terminals, hangars, etc, by the end of the century when the airport is expected to reach saturation point. By that time, annual traffic is expected to be running at 50 million passengers.

In its present form Charles de Gaulle Airport can handle 12 million passengers a year. There is a first, circular *Aerogare* surrounded by seven wedge-shaped satellite terminals, each of which has parking provision for four wide-bodied aircraft. These satellite terminals are reached by a system of tunnels with moving walkways from the main terminal (the *Aerogare*) and which incorporates a four level multi-storey car park capable of accommodating about 4,000 cars. The 11-storey *Aerogare* is the principal terminal facility at CDG, and the original plan provided for the construction of five such buildings, with seven related satellites for each. Some modification of this plan is expected now with future construction, but the need for this development has not yet been reached. For the moment the airport is successfully moving people about by way of escalators and moving walkways through a network of transparent tubes and passageways befitting an airport of the 21st century, let alone the 1980s. Charles de Gaulle Airport is in fact a rather breathtaking space-age airport for the visitor, and seen for the first time can be somewhat overpowering. For all that it is working well, and is in keeping with the era of the Concorde, which flies from the airport to New York and Washington and Rio de Janeiro every week.

The runway plan calls for four parallel runways, each of 11,800ft length (3,600m), but which may be extended to 13,800ft if necessary. The orientation of the first runway, which has been used since commencement of operations in March 1974, is east-west. The associated taxiways produce a total length of 46,000ft. As the high-speed taxiways are 200m (660ft) apart it has been possible to place a slow-speed taxiway between them. There are almost two miles between Runways One and Two, and they are overlooked — as is the whole airport — by one of the world's tallest control towers, an 80m high (262ft) column with the elegantly shaped Navigation Centre at its base.

Top left: Number 1 Aerogare at Charles de Gaulle Airport. The 11-storey radial Aerogare contains four levels for car parking, while other levels accommodate passenger check-in and other services, shops, and restaurants. The seven, wedge-shaped satellite terminals used for flight operations are reached by subterranean channels equipped with moving walkways.

Left: Number One runway at Charles de Gaulle Airport has a present length of 3,600m while extension, ultimately, to 5,000m is possible if required. Runway plan provides for eventual construction of four runways.

Overleaf: Flanked by the airport Air Navigation Centre and ATC complex, and positioned between the first and planned second runways, the 80m control tower is, at the moment, the tallest in Europe.

Perth   Australia

Location: 5.25 miles ENE of Perth
Elevation: 56ft (17m)
Runways in use: 3
02/20 10,310ft × 150ft (3,144m × 45m)
06/24 7,095 ft × 150ft (2,163m × 45m)
11/29 5,766ft × 150ft (1,758m × 45m)
Airport area: 3,526 acres
Passengers handled in 1977: 901,987
Total air transport movements in 1977: 14,690
Cargo handled in 1977: 14,727 tons

Situated on the south-western tip of Australia, and fronting on to the Indian Ocean, is Perth, capital city of Western Australia. The city has a population of just over 800,000 people, and the airport caters for these people together with a further 300,000 who live outside the urban areas but still within the State.

Perth's first airport was at Langley Park, at the edge of the city, and this was used between 1920 and 1923. Maylands Aerodrome, on the banks of the Swan River, was officially opened in January 1924 and was used until 1945, when the present Perth Airport was brought into use at a new site. This site, just over five miles from the city, was first selected in 1938 but delayed in development by World War II, and not introduced into service for commercial traffic until 1945. The first buildings used were those erected for the Royal Australian Air Force, and only

Below: *Down on the south-western tip of Australia, Perth Airport is now handling over 800,000 passengers a year, by wide-bodied jets as well as light twins.*

subsequently did the airlines erect their own hangars and administrative blocks. A brand new passenger terminal, control tower and fire station were erected in October 1962, and since then a customs building has been built and further additions made to the terminal building. The early 1970s dictated also the expansion of the car park to almost twice its previous size, and in 1975 a new international transit lounge was built and integrated with the terminal building at a cost of A$550,000.

The number of movements and passengers handled at Perth has been rising steadily, and from 709 movements in 1948 this had gone up to over 48,000 in 1976. Passenger traffic shot up from 78,000 in 1953 to 854,000 in 1976. Perth is now a regular international stopping place for national airline Qantas, British Airways, Air-India, Singapore Airlines, South African Airways and numerous other operators, including Malaysian Airlines and Cathay Pacific. The airport also provides centralised air traffic control for the region, where there are other airports such as Kalgoorlie and Jandakot, the last of which serves as an airport for flying training, agricultural flying and executive and charter flights. Perth Airport is owned and operated by the Commonwealth Department of Transport.

For the future, the authorities believe that further expansion of the airport will be necessary, and sufficient land has been acquired to permit extension of the main north/south runway (02/20) to a maximum of 14,000ft (4,270m). The likely provision for parallel runways has also been made. The terminal buildings may be further enlarged.

Prague (Ruzyne)   Czechoslovakia

Location: 6.5 miles west of Prague
Elevation: 1,244ft (380m)
Runways in use: 4
31/13 10,660ft x 150ft (3,250m x 45m)
25/07 10,170ft x 150ft (3,100m x 45m)
22/04 7,515ft x 200ft (2,300m x 60m)
26/08 5,480ft x 130ft (1,670m x 40m)
Airport area: 2,023 acres
Passenger handled in 1977: 2,029,457
Total aircraft movements in 1977: 57,685
Cargo handled in 1977: 10,667 tons

The contribution made to aviation by Eastern European countries over the years has been quite strong, and Czechoslovakia is no exception in this respect. The Zlin, Sokol and Aero ranges of light aeroplanes are an example of this contribution and they are enjoyed by pilots in various countries today.

Air transport first came to Czechoslovakia in 1920, when Air France began a service from Paris to Strasbourg and Prague, although the terminating aerodrome was not then Ruzyne but the military airfield at Kbely. The airfield at Kbely served for 16 years as the airfield for both military and civil aircraft, and it was not until 1937 that a move was made to the plain of Ruzyne where a first airport was built. Air services from this new facility actually began on 1 March 1937, just 14 years after Czechoslovakia had been ranked among countries operating their own air services.

During the years between 1933 and 1937 the airport was given what were doubtless thought to be finishing touches to make it one of the best in

Europe, and international recognition of this fact came in 1937 with an award of a gold medal for its construction by the Paris International Exhibition of Arts and Techniques.

The war terminated international air transport services at Prague, but the airport at Ruzyne had been positively established for the day when, in 1946, overseas links with Prague could be resumed. At this point a programme of modernisation was initiated covering the runway system, telecommunications and terminal building extensions. From this point on, development of the airport could not be carried out at a pace equal to the growth of air traffic — a story which has become familiar the world over. In 1937, Prague became a pace'setting airport, and 20 years later the state airline CSA was among the first ICAO member countries to move to the use of jet transports for scheduled services with the introduction of the Russian-built Tu-104. Another 20 years on and Prague Airport was to see operations by the first supersonic airliner to fly, the Tupolev Tu-144.

In the intervening years traffic has climbed in a manner which one might expect of one of the important airports in Europe, and from 1947, when 154,000 people passed through Prague Airport, the

Below: *Prague Airport, with control tower and administrative block in background.*

number of air transport passengers rose to 1,500,000 in 1967 and to 1,977,000 in 1977. Aircraft movements are now in excess of 50,000 a year.

The terminal building was built to handle some four million passengers a year and a corresponding volume of cargo, mail and luggage. It is a steel and concrete skeleton with a steel roof covering, and topped by a 10-storey administrative block. The total floor area covered is five times more than that available at the original Ruzyne Airport.

By western standards the terminal complex is simple and modest in scope, with no system of complicated passenger channelling, but this is no fault, and the existing terminal facilities are pleasantly uncongested for travellers and offer comfort and repose. The terminal building has three quay galleries, two of which also serve as waiting rooms. They are designated as the eastern, western and northern galleries. The circumferential encasement of the building is made of aluminium and glass. Adjacent to the terminal building is the apron and which, prior to enlargement, was the size of Wenceslas Square, Prague.

Another prime building at Ruzyne is the CSA aircraft maintenance hangar. The airport is the headquarters base of Czechoslovak Airlines, which operates a dense domestic airline network, serving 10 key population centres in the country, as well as international services.

Rhodes (Paradissi)   Greece

Location: On the NE coast of Rhodes, 10 miles from the town
Elevation: 200ft (61m)
Runways in use: 1
10,824ft x 150ft (3,300m x 45m)
Passengers handled in 1977: 1,003,058

Total aircraft movements in 1977: 9,998
Cargo handled in 1977: 2,082 tons

Below: *Rhodes' Paradissi Airport, Greece, which was opened newly in the summer of 1977, and is likely to overtake Thessalonika as the second busiest airport in the country.*

The beautiful island of Rhodes, located in the Aegean Sea and just a few miles from the Turkish coast, was given Greece's best looking airport in 1977, when the new airport at Paradissi was opened during the summer.

Preliminary work on the planning of this airport, to replace the old airport at Maritsa, was begun in 1970, and the actual construction work started at the beginning of 1974. Already, 38 airlines are now operating at the airport during the holiday season, and on peak days 13,000 passengers were recorded on 60 flights, including four Jumbos. Paradissi is an airport well-fitted to serve this delightful holiday island, with its smart and spacious halls filtering the wonderful sunshine of the region.

The airport is not only brand new, but the terminal is the largest in Greece, approximately more than double in size the terminals at Corfu and Heraklion, Crete. The passenger halls have a total surface area of over 75,000sq ft and the passenger terminals together have a total length of 820ft. The control tower is the tallest of all the Greek civil airports, at 105ft. At any one time up to 4,000 passengers and personnel can be accommodated in the terminal buildings.

Paradissi Airport was built to handle the increasing tourist traffic to Rhodes, which Maritsa was becoming unable to handle because of the limitations of the terrain which prevented further expansion. Rhodes has been the third busiest airport in Greece, after Athens and Thessalonika, and required enlarged facilities and a longer runway which could handle widebodied aircraft bringing large loads. The group of buildings comprises the main terminal, with two floors and a roof open for spectators and friends of departing passengers; the aircraft control tower building, housing ATC, telecommunications and related services, and a workshop building, which also houses quarters for the technical personnel. Passengers move through one-and-a-half levels, so there is no conflict of traffic nor any impediment of luggage movement. Departing passengers move to the first floor, while arriving passengers use only the ground floor.

The airport buildings are made of reinforced concrete, with faced pillars, and the arched shape of the side towards the town has been designed to give an appearance matching that of the architecture of the island. There are at the moment parking spaces for about 200 cars and 40 buses.

Rio de Janeiro (Galeao)   Brazil

Location: 8 miles NNW of Rio de Janeiro
Elevation: 16ft (5m)
Runways in use: 1
14/32 10,834ft × 150ft (3,300m × 45m)
09/27 13,120ft × 150ft (4,000m × 45m) (under construction)
Passengers handled in 1977: 3,945,000
Total aircraft movements in 1977: 83,000
Cargo handled in 1977: 91,000

The flight around the Eiffel Tower in October 1901 in a powered airship by the Brazilian Alberto Santos-Dumont serves as an illustration of the early interest in flying by the Brazilians, who have made notable strides in commercial aviation since then (Brazil's national airline VARIG is 52 years old). The beautiful city of Rio de Janeiro named its first airport after Santos-Dumont, and in more recent years the second airport at Galeao has been developed to become one of the world's important airports.

Below: *Flanking the Atlantic Ocean, Rio de Janeiro's Galeao Airport is one of the world's newest major airports, yet it is built on the same site as the original Galeao Airport, first used as a joint military/civil airfield. The first of the four half-circle terminal structures is seen here, with the 184ft high control tower at the rear, and placed between the areas for the next terminal development.*

Above: *The landside of Rio's first new terminal complex is shown here, with a clear view of the centrally located 1,400-car park. The control tower has its own access beneath the two bridges of the spine road.*

Galeao is another of the world's water-based airports, and is located on the Rio coast almost in the shadow of the famed Sugarloaf Mountain. It is used by some four million travellers a year, and because of its traffic growth has required considerable enlargement.

Rio has been fortunate in that it has been possible to carry out this modernisation and expansion plan on the site of the existing airport, without recourse to the need to move elsewhere. Long-time travellers to Rio are thus able to continue to fly to the existing site, with the difference that since spring 1977 they have flown to a brand new airport, which was eight years in the planning and construction and which is now open in its first stages.

The development of Rio Airport has been cleverly contrived to make use of the original runway and some existing facilities. There was one original runway and now there are two, and a third runway, parallel to the first, is planned. The new complex of four passenger terminals is located between the two runways and built on the site of some previous facilities. The best possible use is thus made of the land area available, and the life of the site extended for many years ahead — at least up to the year 2000.

The new plan features four terminal buildings, each in a half circle, facing each other in pairs and bisected by a roadway which distributes the traffic to the various buildings. This road system begins at the

original Galeao roadway, and in the future will be connected on the opposite side to the mainland by means of express highways, which are planned by the State of Rio de Janeiro to form a traffic loop, with two airport entries and exits. The terminal buildings are based on the minimum-walking concept, whereby cars may be parked in the car park fronting the terminal, and left by their owners who proceed through the terminal to board waiting aircraft. The aircraft are parked around the airside of the terminal and reached by passenger loading bridges.

Under the design at Rio, arrival and departure flows take place on two levels, with completely independent accesses. After completing the usual travel formalities, departing passengers are directed towards large waiting areas on the upper level. Arriving passengers proceed through health and immigration channels at a mezzanine level between the departures and arrivals levels, and then move to baggage claim, from whence they proceed to the true arrivals level below. This brings them into the arrivals lounge, where they may be met by friends or relatives. On a higher level, and separated from the main passenger levels, are restaurants, bars, cafeteria, duty-free shops, a chapel and an a hotel, as well as telephones and post office facilities and a public panoramic terrace.

An important characteristic of Rio's new passenger terminal complex is its capacity for internal expansion. Whole areas have been left sterile within the building to be brought into use when needed. The car parking area, for example, which in 1978 occupies the ground level, can be increased by the addition of upper levels. The flexible planning is designed to guarantee a service life-term for each building of at least 20 years, and the possibility of multiplying the number of terminals, up to as many as eight, will guarantee the services of the entire airport beyond the year 2000. At the moment there is one half circular terminal. There will be four by 1990.

The existing runway and the new runway under construction (09/27) form an open V and constitute a system which will be sufficient for traffic up to 1990. A third runway, laid parallel to the original strip, will raise the capacity of the airport further, and for operational needs beyond 2000. Runway 09/27 will be over 13,000ft long and equipped for Category II operations. The apron areas will cover over 3,000,000sq ft. The present terminal apron will provide 13 aircraft positions reached by telescoping bridges, and 19 remote parking positions. With four terminals in operation this number of parking positions will be multiplied accordingly. The terminal complex is overseen by a 184ft high control tower, located between Terminals One and Two, and equipped with the most modern aids including ILS, DME, VDF, VOR and primary and secondary radars.

Rome (Leonardo da Vinci Intercontinental)   Italy

Location: 19 miles SW of Rome
Elevation: 6.5ft (2m)
Runways in use: 3
16L/34R 12,790ft x 200ft (3,900m x 60m)
07/25 10,824ft x 200ft (3,300m x 60m)
16R/34L 12,790ft x 200ft (3,900m x 60m)
Airport area: 3,532 acres
Passengers handled in 1977: 10,472,687
Total air transport movements in 1977: 142,095
Cargo handled in 1977: 153,547 tons

Rome's intercontinental airport of Fiumicino adjoins the coastal town and fronts on to the Tyrrhenian sea. It was built to replace the previously used Ciampino Airport, and opened for international services in 1961. The plans were the work of the Ministry of Air Defence, while the airport was built by the Italian Ministry of Public Works. As the national airline, Alitalia had a hand in the planning of much of the terminal facilities. Then, as now, Rome's new airport had great potential for expansion because it was built on an extensive area of flat terrain, which was of course also important insofar as it presented no natural obstacles to flight.

Officially named Leonardo da Vinci Intercontinental, after the Italian aeronautical and mechanical genuis of the 16th century, the airport was endowed with attractive contouring which did justice to some of the artistry of its namesake. The international terminal building is, in essence, a large hall with a front walkway developing into natural piers on either side. Passengers reach the apron by means of short walkways and ramps projecting from the piers. The terminal hall is spacious, measuring 600ft x 400ft, and the natural piers on either side are also very wide, with plenty of room for movement and waiting. The ramps from the piers lead down to the apron from where the traveller either walks to his waiting aircraft or takes an airside bus to the aircraft parking point. The weather at Rome usually guarantees that this is an acceptable procedure.

When first opened, the airport handled what was then regarded as the imposing figure of 2.5 million passengers a year. Over the years the traffic through Leonardo da Vinci Intercontinental has swollen to 10.5 million passengers a year or over four times the original figure, and terminal extensions and additions have become increasingly necessary. The most recent of these was the creation of a new domestic services terminal, built to the side of the north-

Below: Airside view of Leonardo da Vinci Airport, Rome's new domestic passenger terminal, which has been integrated with the international building on the right, to facilitate interlining. Unlike the international terminal, the new domestic building has no passenger ramps down to the apron, passengers being carried by apron buses to the aircraft.

Above: *Interior of domestic arrivals hall in new passenger terminal at Rome.*

easterly pier, and specifically for the handling of passengers within Italy. This building, like its predecessor domestic terminal at the airport, was designed by Alitalia, whose subsidary airline, Aero Trasporti Italiani (ATI) carries the bulk of Italian domestic passenger traffic. Because of the interlining that ensues at the airport it was considered desirable to integrate the new terminal with the original building, and this has been done in a manner designed to ensure smooth flow of arriving, departing and transiting passengers.

The terminal has a length of approximately 350yd and all passenger processing takes place on the ground floor. The check-in counters for departing passengers are arranged in two islands of 10 counters each in the centre of the building, while there are four more counters for standby passengers. In the domestic departures area, to the right-hand side of the building, there are 14 gates, arranged on either side of the check-in counters. There is a central security check facility at the entrance of each group of gates. Passing through this security check, passengers enter a broad corridor equipped with seats, as the next move in leaving for their aircraft. These are reached by airside buses, which leave directly from outside of the lounge doors.

In this new passenger terminal, passenger loading bridges have been dispensed with, partly because there is just insufficient parking place for aircraft on the airside of this terminal; the idea of extending passenger piers from the face of the terminal was also considered as achieving little from the point of view of passenger facilitation while adding substantially to building costs.

For arriving passengers, arrivals are made at the same ground level, and on the left-hand side of the terminal. Passengers from domestic flights enter through one set of gates, while passengers on international flights enter through another. Passengers on a domestic flight but travelling onwards to a foreign destination, take escalators to an upper floor for movement to the adjoining international terminal. Travellers on domestic flights within Italy take a subway on the landside of the terminal into the domestic departures area. There are information and service counters for both sets of passengers in the various halls on their route.

The new passenger terminal at Rome has been designed to handle domestic traffic at the airport at least until the end of the 1980s. With domestic travellers now running at 3.5 million passengers a year the capacity of this terminal is calculated as being approximately seven million passengers a year.

While located 19 miles to the south-west of Rome, Leonardo da Vinci is served by frequent airport bus services.

Rotterdam (Zestienhoven)   Holland

Location: 3.5 miles NW of Rotterdam
Elevation: 13ft (4m) below sea level
Runways in use: 1
06/24 7,216ft × 150ft (2,200m × 45m)
Passengers handled in 1976: 313,000
Total aircraft movements in 1976: 8,000
Cargo handled in 1976: 10,000 tons

Rotterdam Airport will hold memories for many travellers of the early postwar years who flew on the car ferry services operated to the Dutch city from Southend by Air Charter Limited — an airline operated by a gentleman now called Sir Freddie Laker. The airport had by then been re-built following its destruction in the war. Like the city it serves, Rotterdam Airport was to rise again after the war in new fashion.

A further facelift was given in 1971 with the construction of a fine new terminal topped by a neat control tower. Apart from the basic passenger facilities of restaurant, money-changing counters and ticketing and information desks, the car parks were enlarged and bus and taxi services increased.

In the mid-1970s , the idea of a second major airport for the Netherlands was given greater currency, and because of this the future of Rotterdam Airport was suddenly put in doubt. One school of thought suggested that if a second major airport was built, Rotterdam Airport should be closed down, and its existing traffic transferred to Schiphol, Amsterdam.

The suggested second major airport for Holland has not advanced in the planning, and may not do so, but whether it does or not Rotterdam Airport is unlikely to be closed, for the airport is an important traffic hub and air freighting centre, and is said to fulfil a crucial role. The local Chamber of Commerce and the Rotterdam Port Employers' Association believe strongly in the airport's future, and point out that some 200 tons of air freight are generated every day in the Rotterdam region. The Rotterdam Airport Authority sees an even greater future for the airport than at present, and is confident that international services will be operated there for many years. The airport is used by numerous operators today in addition to national airline KLM. The airport is used by propeller-driven aircraft and noise-certificated jet aircraft 24 hours a day. A night curfew operates between 23.30 and 06.00 for uncertificated jet aircraft.

As Holland's second city, Rotterdam has an airport which offers much potential to certain types of operators, and it is to be hoped that this potential is fully realised.

Below: *Rotterdam Airport serves the second city of the Netherlands, although traffic is modest.*

Seattle International (Sea-Tac)   USA

Location: 13 miles south of Seattle, 20 miles from Tacoma, Washington State
Elevation: 428ft (130m)
Runways in use: 2
16L/34R 11,900ft × 150ft (3,660m × 45m)
16R/34L 9,425ft × 150ft (2,872m × 45m)
Airport area: 2,100 acres
Passengers handled in 1977: 7,332,443
Total aircraft movements in 1977: 190,026
Cargo tonnage handled in 1977: 191,603 tons

In air transport circles Seattle, in Washington State, is noted for being the home of the mighty Boeing company, and is so geared to aviation that all the local schools have courses in aeronautics.

Not surprisingly for this busy city, the international airport of Seattle-Tacoma, generally known as Sea-Tac, handles many aviation-orientated visitors among its annual throughput of more than seven million travellers, although as an important seaport and grain centre many of the visitors are on other business too.

Owned and operated by the Port of Seattle, authority to undertake airport activities was first

Below: The main 11,900ft runway at Seattle-Tacoma is flanked by the shorter parallel runway, and which both run to a wooded area with a lake (Lake Reba) to the north and a golf course and the fuel farm to the south.

granted in 1941, and land acquisition and the first airport construction work was started in 1942. While Boeing had had its own aerodrome at Seattle for years, the civil airport did not actually commence airline operations until 1947, and then on the modest basis of 10 flights a day by two airlines. Today there are over 400 flights a day operated by 12 airlines.

The growth of traffic at Seattle-Tacoma has been very much a postwar surge and in particular in the last 10 years, when traffic has grown to such a degree that the airport now ranks among the top 24 airports world-wide in numbers of passengers annually passing through. This is, perhaps, one of the most significant things about Sea-Tac, although there are others, not the least of which was the introduction by the airport in 1972 of one of the first inter-terminal airport transit systems for passengers.

Because of the recent growth, the Port of Seattle undertook a $175 million construction and re-modelling programme at the airport, and which was completed in 1973. Insofar as any airport construction programme is completed, this left Sea-Tac with a passenger handling capability for 12 million passengers annually. Eventually the airport expects to be handling efficiently 15 million travellers a year, which will place it among the busiest US airports.

The airport today is not beautiful but it is certainly functional and has a number of interesting features,

one of which is the incorporation of two remote, satellite terminals, which passengers reach by underground passageway from the main building. These terminals have provision for parking of up to eight big aircraft around them, and support the operations from the piers on the north and south concourses. Their location on the apron, separate from the main building and in a 'sea' of concrete, also gives a clear taxying space for aircraft all around them, and eliminates the congestion of nose-in terminal parking at a main building. The arrangement also keeps down the noise level in the main terminal.

Seattle-Tacoma is an innovative airport, and amongst its innovations is the inter-terminal transit system (another has been the introduction of selected pieces of public art in the passenger terminals, which include Pacific Rim artefacts from the Burke Museum of the University of Washington). The Satellite Transit System consists of 9,050 feet of underground railway which connects the main passenger terminal with the north and south satellites. The system has two separate loops, with the south loop beginning in the main terminal and ending at the end of Concourse B, the pier projecting from the main terminal. En route, it serves the south satellite terminal. The north loop begins in the main terminal, makes stops at the north satellite terminal, and concludes at Concourse C, the northerly pier. There is also a shuttle beneath the main terminal which connects the two loops.

As a 'people-moving' system, the Sea-Tac STS is said to be one of the most efficient in the USA, with a reliability factor of 99%. Made by Westinghouse

Above: Schematic of the Seattle-Tacoma Satellite Transit System is seen in background, and airport layout diagram at right. The 'people-moving' STS is monitored from the control point.

Overleaf: Visible here are Seattle-Tacoma's two remoted satellite terminals. The STS runs beneath the apron serving all concourses.

Electric, the system has 12, 106-passenger vehicles running automatically over the network and serving eight stations altogether. The STS runs underground to free the aprons and surface for aircraft and ground support equipment, while providing a ready means of connection between the terminals for travellers. In 1976 these travellers numbered 9,304,984, or almost three million more passengers than used the airport on flights. The automatic operation is supervised by a central control computer, which controls station standing times and places the trains correctly in the system at all times.

Seattle-Tacoma Airport has its problems, not the least of which is warm fog, very prevalent in the region. This fog covers areas above the freezing point, and is more difficult to disperse than cold fog. In 1976 Sea-Tac suffered its worst fog season in 20 years, and as a way of dispersing it airlines at the airport carried out an intensified programme of fog seeding. This programme is maintained at the airport, but in October, November and December of the year seeding was done on 25 days altogether, and it was estimated that 289 carriers that might not have landed were able to do so as a result of the work. Category II ILS is installed at Sea-Tac. Another

of the airport's problems has been aircraft noise, and Sea-Tac has been meeting this problem head-on with a relocation programme which, while costly, has been very successful, both for the residents of the area and the Port of Seattle. The programme began in 1975 with assistance provided by the Federal Aviation Administration under the ADAP plan (Airport Development Aid Program), which enabled the Port to buy land along the airport perimeter from the owners at an independently appraised value. Once the owners were satisfied with the sums being offered, they began buying alternative accommodation and turned their properties over to the Port, which in most cases physically moved them from the area and smoothed and replanted the land. The programme, has been continuing, along with other moves aimed at noise reduction.

These difficulties aside, Seattle-Tacoma Intercontinental serves as an important traffic hub, provides employment for many thousands of people, and makes a profit for its operators.

Shannon International   Ireland

Location: 12 miles WNW of Limerick
Elevation: 46ft (14m)
Runways in use: 1
06/24 10,500ft × 150ft (3,200m × 45m)
Passengers handled in 1977: 1,175,700
Total aircraft movements in 1977: 43,000
Cargo handled in 1977: 11,000 tonnes

The development of Shannon International Airport into the busy traffic terminal that it is today is a story of Irish enterprise worth recording. It owes a lot to the familiarity of the Irish with past adversities, out of which has come many strengths.

Between the first scheduled commercial transatlantic flight through Shannon in October 1945 and commencement of the first North Atlantic long-range jet services in 1958, approximately 80% of North Atlantic traffic stopped for refuelling at

Shannon. The airport offered a prime location for business. A major catering and sales organisation was built up around the airport, and by 1951 Shannon had become a Customs-free airport and opened what is claimed to be the world's first duty-free airport stores. From this store concept a mail order business was generated, and further innovations followed. By the end of the 1950s Shannon Airport was a major centre of employment on the Irish west coast, with a workforce of 2,000 people.

With the introduction of the big long-range jets the prosperity of the airport was threatened, for with the diminishing need for refuelling services, the number of aircraft calling at Shannon looked like relegating the airport to one of secondary importance on the North Atlantic routes. As a major national investment and asset, the airport was in need of a promotional plan, and the Irish Government came up with this in the form of the Shannon Free Airport Development Company, which was established in 1959 as a means of bringing the over-flying jets down from the sky.

Below: Terminal building with pier and airbridges at Shannon International. In background is Shannon River estuary.

The strategy was to extend the duty-free zone and to establish Shannon as a major air freight centre, and also to develop the volume of passenger traffic through the airport by promoting it as a gateway to the tourist attractions in the mid-west region of Ireland. In 1959 the first factory units were erected on what is claimed to have been the world's first airport duty-free industrial park. The Shannon Airport Development Company offered overseas companies a pool of available labour, low rates, government-backed training schemes and the air-freighting facility of the airport.

The scheme worked, and by 1976 Shannon had over 40 manufacturing firms and an equal number of warehousing and service companies employing over 4,000 people in the industrial park adjoining the airport. Freight traffic through the airport grew from 100 tonnes yearly in 1960 to 10,000 tonnes by 1975. The growth of industry at Shannon created the need for a reservoir of labour close to the industrial zones, and in 1961 the first buildings were constructed for the first new town in Ireland for over two centuries. By 1975 the population of the new town of Shannon had grown to over 7,000.

Passenger traffic was growing as a result of the new activity around the airport, and a campaign of tourism promotion was embarked upon in the early 1960s. Bunratty, Knappogue and Dunguaire castles were opened for mediaeval banquets, folk parks were established, and museums and collections were improved and made available to tourists. These facilities were promoted in concert with the airport's duty-free shops, and then Shannon Castle Tours and Irish rent-a-cottage organisations joined the marketing efforts.

The result of all of this inspiration and work has been an impressive growth in the passenger traffic through Shannon Airport, as hoped for, and from the 407,000 people that passed through the airport in 1958 — only one-fifth of whom were terminal passengers — over a million passengers used the airport in 1975; in 1977 this traffic rose further to 1,175,000. Of these, 552,000 were terminal passengers, that is, passengers using the airport specifically to visit other areas.

Today, the airport has parking provisions for 19 aircraft, with access to the terminal by piers and airbridges, has restaurants, lounges and all the usual airport facilities, operates on a 24-hour basis with no night-time curfew for noise abatement, and is once again firmly on the map as an air port of call for airlines from North America and elsewhere.

Sharjah International   UAE

Location: 6 miles ESE of Sharjah
Elevation: 114ft (35m)
Runways in use: 1
12/30 12,333ft × 150ft (3,760m × 45m)
Passengers handled in 1977: 60,351
Total aircraft movements in 1977: 7,049
Cargo handled in 1977: 8,402 tons

Below: *Officially opened in its first stage on 1 January 1977, the Arab Emirate airport at Sharjah has a uniquely different set of airport buildings which reflect the character of the region. A trio of mosque-like terminals are flanked by a slender control tower.*

In 1932 an agreement was signed by the then ruler of Sharjah and the British Government for the establishment of an 'air station'. In those days this state on the Persian Gulf was regarded by Imperial Airways as a stopping point on the new road to India, and by 1936 passengers could spend the night in a real desert fort on their way from Australia to London. Now a member of the United Arab Emirates, Sharjah is a booming Gulf commercial centre. Largely as a result of the development of the oil refining business, Sharjah is a fast-growing state in the UAE.

On 1 January 1977 the one-time air station gave way to a magnificent new international airport with the official opening of the completed Sharjah International. Linked to the sea ports of Sharjah and Khor Fakkan as well as a new trans-Arabian trucking terminal, the airport has been made a crucial part of 'Sharjahport', the Gulf's first intermodal transport location.

For connoisseurs of airport design, the new airports of the Gulf region are among the most attractive currently being built anywhere in the world, and Sharjah International is no exception, with its trio of mosque-like terminal buildings flanked by a slender control tower. In its first stage, the airport has provision for three B747 types plus two narrow-bodied aircraft, and the cargo apron space for one B747 type and one narrow-bodied type. Ultimately, there will be space for six wide-bodied jets on the main passenger aprons and the cargo terminal area will be able to provide for nine large aircraft in total; a container/distribution terminal area adjoining the cargo facility will also have ramp provision for nine large aircraft. Air cargo is given special attention at Sharjah, and air cargo specialists Deutsche Lufthansa and the Frankfurt Airport Authority have been retained as air cargo advisers and managers at the airport.

Sharjah was in fact largely planned by the consulting division of the Frankfurt Airport Authority, which manages the airport today under a contract with the Sharjah Airport Authority. The British company International Aeradio is providing technical services at the airport under a similar contract, and which services include air traffic control, communications, fire and rescue, technical maintenance, operational management, and aircraft ground handling. The company had previously supplied navigational aids, fire fighting and ground handling equipment.

While the airport is seen as an important new business facility, with an ultimate capacity for 10 million passengers a year, Sharjah itself is regarded by its government as a centre for great tourist activity, for at its location on the Gulf the state offers sandy beaches, rugged mountains and green oases, as well as the desert. There are also numerous hotels provided by well-known chains from England, France, India and the USA, offering over 4,000 rooms for visitors. To develop the tourist potential the Government of Sharjah has retained Lufthansa Consulting, a division of the West German airline.

The airport is open 24 hours a day, and is currently being used by 15 airlines.

Singapore (Paya Lebar/Changi)

PAYA LEBAR
Location: 7 miles east of the City of Singapore
Elevation: 66ft (20m)
Runways in use: 1
02/20 13,200ft × 200ft (4,023m × 60m)
Passengers handled in 1977: 5,078,648
Total aircraft movements in 1977: 66,950
Cargo handled in 1977: 86,000 tonnes

CHANGI
Location: On easterly tip of Singapore 16 miles from the city
Runways: 2
Parallel, 13,120ft × 200ft (4,000m × 60m)
11,000ft × 200ft (3,355m × 60m)
Airport area: 3,992 acres
Airport to be opened in December 1980

The island of Singapore, in the South China Sea and just about a mile off the south end of the Malay Peninsula, is remarkable for the place it has earned in the world as a trading centre and international hub of business and commerce. Apart from the great progress the island republic has made in guiding its own destiny since independence in 1965, the former British Crown Colony has developed its trading and business skills to a fine art, and is now a world focal point for banking, insurance and currency exchange as well as a 'supermarket' for world goods. Some 59% of the products made in the Republic are exported, and the port of Singapore (one of the world's four busiest) is used by over 150 major shipping lines. Additionally, Singapore is one of the world's largest oil refining, blending and distributing centres, is a major world supplier of electronic components and a centre for shipbuilding and repairing.

The international airport has consequently become ever-more important to the country as this trading status has grown, and a rich variety of visitors on all kinds of missions is seen at the airport today. The traffic through the airport has literally soared, from 250,000 in 1958, to just under a million in 1966, to over 2.5 million in 1972, and to a remarkable five million just five years later, in 1977. Not surprisingly, the present and long-serving airport of Paya Lebar is almost at the limit of its capacity, and will be supplanted in 1980 by a brand new

Top right: Pilot's eye view of the runway at Paya Lebar, Singapore, approaching from the south. Terminal complex is on the left.

Right: Operations block and control tower at Paya Lebar Airport, Singapore. The new airport at Changi, which will take over from Paya Lebar in 1980, will feature a control centre equipped with S$100 million-worth of radar and electronics.

international airport at Changi. This airport is well into construction as this is being written. It will be five times bigger than Paya Lebar.

The airport at Paya Lebar, located to the east on the island and seven miles from the city, was originally used by Britain as the principal Royal Air Force base in the Far East, but this role declined as the RAF's base at Changi was developed into an important military aerodrome. The operations at Paya Lebar gradually became almost entirely commercial, until a dozen airlines were using the airport in 1960 and big jet operations were routine.

Substantial development work took place in the early 1960s, and the hangars used by the military were modified and converted into a spacious passenger terminal. In time, travel facilities such as banking, postal and money exchanges were introduced, together with shops and a public restaurant. A new operations block was built in 1960, and in September 1961 the Area Control Centre was transferred to this permanent location. A new passenger terminal took its place alongside the operations block, and largely by a process of evolution, Paya Lebar became a good international airport.

The single runway was lengthened steadily, from 8,000 to 9,000ft, then to 11,000ft and a further extension programme took it to the present 13,200ft, to make it among the longest in the world. Related threshold and apron improvement work was done, and an ILS installed.

As the traffic grew, it was necessary to carry out more terminal improvement work even as the plans for a new airport were being approved, and a new Arrivals Building was put into operation in December 1977. This cost S$3.5 million, and provided for travellers a single storey steel portal frame structure 1,155ft long by 190ft across. A new air freight terminal was built also, and a hangar capable of accommodating the largest wide-bodied aircraft. There are now 30 scheduled airlines using Singapore Airport, and this terminal and other work has been very necessary.

The limits to expansion at Paya Lebar became clear in the early 1970s when the traffic was already doubling itself rapidly. The island of Singapore is only 26 miles long by 14 miles wide, and space is at a premium in this tiny republic. The only prospect for a widening of air transport facilities, therefore, was to look at the idea of a new airport site altogether, rather than trying to struggle along with the existing airport.

To be known as Changi International Airport, the new facility was formally approved by the Singapore Government in June 1975 and land reclamation for the airport began in April 1976. The airport location is partially on the site of the former RAF base, at the eastern tip of the island, but should be easier to reach by car than the present airport because two roads will be constructed specifically for the airport; these will be ready in time for the terminal opening.

By the time of the opening of the first facilities — scheduled for December 1980 — passenger traffic at Singapore is expected to be running at about 6.4 million a year, and the first terminals at Changi will be able to handle about 10 million passengers a year. If traffic reaches 10.5 million a year by 1982, as thought likely, a second passenger terminal with a similar capacity will be built. Space is being reserved, in fact, for third and fourth passenger terminals should expansion be required by the end of the century, when annual passenger throughput might be some 30 million passengers a year.

Much of the land that will be taken up by the new airport is being reclaimed from the sea, and some is also former swampland. Appropriately enough, perhaps, a Dutch firm of airport planners and consultants (NACO) has been responsible for the overall project, while the actual land reclamation work has been undertaken by a Japanese firm of hydraulic engineers under the supervision of the Singapore Port Authority.

The principal terminal at Changi will be a five-storey structure costing some S$250 million. It will have two parallel fingers, each 1,900ft long. Work began on the foundations of this terminal in June 1977. The terminal — and its later fellows — will be equipped with moving walkways for passengers, new baggage conveyor systems, and airbridges for boarding the aircraft from the terminal. In the first phase 22 airbridges will be installed and another eight later. In addition to these 30 aircraft stands near the terminal there will be another 15 remoted stands. A hydrant fuelling system will be installed, and up to 80 aircraft movements an hour will be possible.

There will be two parallel runways, with the longest of 13,120ft (4,000m) length, based upon the military runway and lengthened from 2,500m. The new control tower and related ATC buildings is being built on what is known as Biggin Hill, and when outfitted will incorporate S$100 million of equipment. This will include radar capable of picking up supersonic aircraft at a range of over 200 miles.

Below: *The information counter in the passenger terminal building at Singapore.*

Taipei (Taipei International/Taoyuan) Taiwan

TAIPEI INTERNATIONAL
Location: 3 miles NE of city centre
Elevation: 22ft (6.7m)
Runways in use: 1
10/28 8,520ft × 200ft (2,597m × 60m)
Passengers handled in 1977: 6,219,159
Total aircraft movements in 1977: 66,327
Cargo handled in 1977: 127,959 tons

TAOYUAN
Location: 25 miles from Taipei railway station
Elevation: 108ft (33m)
Runways: 5/23 First phase 12,000ft × 200ft
(3,658m × 60m)
5R/23L Second phase 10,500ft × 200ft
(3,200m × 60m)
Airport area: 2,965 acres
Airport scheduled to be opened end 1978

Above: *Taipei International Airport is currently
handling 10,000 arriving and departing passengers
daily. The main terminal is fronted by an attractive
plaza, with playing fountains.*

Civil Aeronautics Administration of the Ministry of
Communications, and this office is responsible for
the construction, operation and management of the
airport. From 1965 air transport to and from Taiwan
began to grow rapidly, and an enlargement and
modernisation programme was put in hand to deal
with the growing pressure on space. The annual
growth rate of traffic was rising at an average of
21.8% or 6.5 times that of a decade before.

It is this sort of growth which has led to the
construction of a new airport to take the pressure
from Taipei International, and this airport was
scheduled to be completed by the end of 1978. The
new airport has been designed to handle traffic up to
the year 2000. Like its predecessor, the airport is
located in the north of the country, but rather further
from the city, and is 25 miles from Taipei railway
station. A four-lane, five-mile long access road
connects the airport with the TIA interchange of the
freeway to the city, and makes for fast connection.
The site of the airport is on a plain not far from the
coast, on what was agricultural land. The site is
known as Taoyuan, and the airport will therefore be
known as Taoyuan International Airport.

When completed the new airport will occupy
almost 3,000 acres and have 10 operational areas,
which can be categorised as aircraft operations,
passenger terminal complex, control tower and flight
operations, cargo terminal, aircraft maintenance,
flight kitchen, fuel storage, airmail processing,
telecommunications and airport hotel and
administrative services. It will have two runways and
a capability for handling 10 million passengers
annually by 1990.

Taiwan's third airport is Kaohsiung International,
which is to continue supporting the other two.

The 250-mile long island of Taiwan, located 100
miles east of the Chinese mainland and previously
known as Formosa, is still something of a political
curiosity with its title of the 'Republic of China'. The
country has, however, developed in the last few
years to become one of the most commercially
industrious on earth, and for this reason it already
has two airports handling civil traffic and will soon
have a third, brand new one.

Taipei is the capital city, with a population of over
two million, and its airport is situated north-east of
the city, approximately three miles from the centre. It
is the hub of air transport in the country, and handles
over 180 domestic and international flights daily,
with arriving and departing passengers averaging
10,000.

The Taipei International Airport Office was
established in March 1950 under jurisdiction of the

Tokyo (Narita)   Japan

Location: Narita city, Chiba Prefecture, 41 miles east of Tokyo
Elevation: 135ft (41m)
Runways in use: 1
16R/34L 13,120ft × 200ft (4,000m × 60m)
Other runways:
16L/34R 8,200ft × 200ft (2,500m × 60m)
03/21 10,500ft × 200ft (3,200m × 60m)
Airport area: 2,630 acres
Airport opened May 1978

Probably no airport that has been constructed in the last few years received so much adverse publicity as did Narita Airport up to the time it was opened for flights in May 1978. The airport was built to serve Tokyo, although it is a good distance from the city (41 miles), a fact that has always been one of its less attractive features for passengers and airlines; however, it was political rather than air transport problems, which gave the airport its bad name.

Narita was conceived in 1965 when the Japanese Ministry of Transport made an intensive investigation of 20 possible airport sites in the Tokyo area in the search for a replacement for Haneda. The island airport of Haneda, located in Tokyo Bay, had long ago been seen to be congested and with no potential for future development, and Narita finally emerged as the best possible replacement. In July 1966 the Japanese Government designated the Sanrizuka area of Narita city as the site for Tokyo's new airport. Narita is one of 36 cities in Chiba province.

Right from the start of the major construction work, which was commenced in 1970, Narita experienced opposition to its creation, firstly from environmental and pressure groups, but then later on an organised scale by hostile, anti-airport factions and political agitators, who claimed to speak for the world at large. For its part, the Tokyo International Airport Corporation maintained that fears by local residents about safety and noise pollution could be dispelled, and that negotiations for the purchase of most of the private land required for the airport were satisfactorily settled by the original date set for opening. This was set for the beginning of 1974, but arguments over remaining pieces of land were amplified and exaggerated by political extremists to the degree that official opening of the new airport was delayed for four years.

Once open, however, Narita Airport offered modern facilities for both passengers and airline personnel. For passenger processing the airport has been designed with north and south wings to a main terminal building, the wings designed to function independently. The north wing is used by Japan Air Lines and a number of foreign airlines handled by JAL, and the south wing is used by other foreign airlines. Both wings have two separate satellite terminals with parking spaces for seven aircraft, to provide in total parking places for 28 aircraft at one time. Each wing has separate inspection areas for immigration and customs formalities, while the central building houses restaurants, shops, offices and observation decks. Car parking places are also available, for up to 12,000 cars. The first and second floors in the terminals are designated for arriving passengers, while the third and fourth floors handle departing passengers. Priority was given to making this passenger flow smooth and without conflict. When Narita Airport was first planned, Haneda was already handling 4.5 million passengers a year and a replacement airport was considered vital by 1975. In 1976, because of the delays, the old airport was being obliged to handle almost 18 million passengers annually in wildly overcrowded conditions. In its first stages of development Narita was designed to handle up to 16 million passengers a year.

From the traffic projections it is clear that a new airport was necessary to handle the massive traffic passing through the Tokyo area, and the planners of the New Tokyo International Airport Corporation were determined to give careful attention to the matter of passenger processing. Apart from ensuring easy passenger access to any part of the buildings, even without signposting, they made psychological studies to determine behaviour patterns and emotional requirements of passengers and those accompanying them, and the results of these studies were employed in the architectural design of the terminal.

Arriving passengers enter the central hall of the appropriate satellite through a covered boarding bridge. They continue along the pier to the quarantine and immigration posts, and then downstairs to the baggage claim carousels. Departing passengers enter one of the wings of the terminal from a special approach road which leads to the kerbside entrance. They pass through ticket and baggage processing at one of the check-in islands and then proceed to the departure lobby, which commands a fine view of the aprons on the airside. The aircraft are reached by the passenger loading bridges.

In its first stage, Narita has two satellite terminals in use and one main runway, but it will ultimately have three runways, the longest being 13,120ft long. There will also be provision for an eventual 96 aircraft parking places. In its first stage Narita should be capable of handling 410,000 tons of cargo annually; eventually it should have capacity for 1,400,000 tons a year.

Because of its great distance from the heart of Tokyo a number of systems of access were planned. These included an expressway and a high speed train service directly to the capital. At the time of writing the bullet-train service direct to the airport was not operating, and the airport bus service was the most convenient. This runs between Tokyo City Air

Top right: *The main runway at Narita, showing, on the right, the terminal complex with satellite buildings.*

Right: *Tokyo's Narita Airport had a chequered history of false starts before it was officially opened to passenger traffic in mid-1978. This is the imposing, if unlovely, control tower and operations centre.*

Left: *Testing the HSST.*

Terminal and the airport and takes about 80 minutes journey-time, depending upon the traffic. Railway trains run from north-east Tokyo to the Keisei Airport Station, which is a few hundred yards from the Narita Airport passenger terminal.

A high speed train service is also planned however, and this system, called HSST (High Speed Surface Transport) has been under development by Japan Air Lines, which has invested a great deal of its own money in research, a test track and the construction of several test vehicles to date. The HSST is powered by an electric linear induction motor, and which propels the vehicle along the track by magnetic levitation. In tests up to the middle of 1978 trains had reached speeds of over 180mph.

Toronto International (Malton)   Canada

Location: 17 miles from Toronto
Elevation: 569ft (173m)
Runways in use: 4
14/32 11,050ft × 200ft (3,367m × 60m)
05R/23L 9,500ft × 200ft (2,895m × 60m)
10/28 3,400ft × 200ft (1,035m × 60m)
05L/23R 10,500ft × 200ft (3,200m × 60m)
Airport area: 14,000 acres
Passengers handled in 1977: 12,305,000
Total air transport movements in 1977: 175,700
Cargo handled in 1977: 150,000 tons

Canada has been placing increasing emphasis upon airport facilities in recent years, and recognition of the greater importance of airports has been manifest in projects such as the new airport for Montreal at Mirabel, the decision to market Canadian airport planning and construction expertise in countries overseas, and the formation of airport consultancy consortia able to offer to interested parties complete airports on a turnkey basis.

It was not always so. Canadian air transport really got under way only in the 1930s, and the important city of Toronto then had five relatively small grass airfields to handle the traffic. A larger airport became a requirement with the establishment of the government-sponsored Trans-Canada Air Lines (now Air Canada) in April 1937, and the first moves towards selecting a site for this airport were made in 1936. As T-CA was being given official blessing, the Department of Transport and the Toronto Harbour Commission were in process of deciding upon the site for Toronto's new airport, at Malton, 17 miles from the heart of the city and deep in Canadian farmland. The authorities could not know that 40 years later the Toronto area would generate the greatest number of air passenger trips among all metropolitan areas in Canada.

The first passenger terminal at Toronto Airport was a converted farmhouse, and this building served also as the administration centre, the operations hub and the weather office combined. It was to serve as a passenger terminal until 1939, when a new, wood-framed building was erected, and this in turn served, with various additions, until 1949.

The modern brick and steel terminal which took over was twice enlarged, to double both its length and width, before a problem arose which led to a completely fresh approach to providing for passengers. Simply, this problem was the growth in traffic, which had risen from 300,000 passengers in 1949 to 1,700,000 by the late 1950s. As improvisations were made to accommodate the passengers and the aircraft passenger walking distance grew from 300ft to 1,500ft and facilities grew ever more separated. Studies were commenced on the design for a new terminal in 1956, and the planning of this began in the autumn of 1957.

The structure which was to result was a building separated from the administration building and the airline workshops: it was a strikingly original airport terminal concept. Known as the Aeroquay, and today known as Terminal 1, the structure was a complete passenger terminal housing all facilities for travellers and nothing else. This included ticketing and processing areas, Customs halls, coffee shops and a restaurant, newstands and shops, spectators' galleries and a seven-storey car park with a capacity for 2,400 cars. Airport management functions and air traffic control were completely excluded from this building to leave the Aeroquay free for its intended purpose of serving as a passenger terminal. The facility was opened for use in February 1964, and cost $30 million.

The circular concept of the Aeroquay was designed to minimise passenger walking distances, to allow speed of service, provide protection from aircraft noise and offer convenient car parking facilities. In these aims the Aeroquay initially succeeded, for as a remoted facility placed in the centre of the apron, the terminal was removed from concentrated aircraft noise, and gave passengers ready access to the aircraft (by airbridges) and also to their cars, which they simply parked in the multi-storey box-shaped central core.

As airport authorities using island sites have come to discover, however, there are limitations on the practicalities of such designs in the fast-moving world of air transport, and Toronto Airport (now owned and operated by the federal government through the Canadian Air Transportation Administration) soon experienced problems. The first of these was the congestion caused by visitors to the airport in their cars. Sightseers caused exit delays from the car park of up to 2½ hours, and clogged the access tunnels to the Aeroquay for airline travellers, thus reducing its effectiveness.

The number of passengers using the airport grew at a faster rate than anticipated and the airport operators were obliged to make modifications to the existing Aeroquay even before they were ready to construct another. Such a plan was in mind, dependent upon the success of Aeroquay 1. Originally designed to handle 3.2 million passengers annually, the Aeroquay has now been modified several times to increase its capacity to five million passengers annually. Serious overcrowding of passengers was experienced before long, and by 1970 it was clear there were insufficient gates for wide-bodied aircraft. The holding rooms were proving to be undersized for the task that would be required of them, and general limitations for future expansion were increasingly apparent with the Aeroquay concept.

The result of this was the reversion to linear type design by the planners when a second terminal, to be known as Terminal 2, was put into construction. This building is a straightforward rectangular structure adjoining the administration area and close to the airport approach roads, and embodying few, if any, notable design features. In comparison with the Aeroquay it is depressingly dull, but it does have possibilities for expansion, and in this respect Terminal 2 will probably serve its purpose better than Terminal 1. It came into service first in June 1972, when Stage One was opened, and Stage Two was introduced into use in April 1973, when Air Canada transferred its entire operations from Terminal 1. Stage Three in the terminal's construction was scheduled to be completed and fully operational in late 1978. This stage comprised a 750ft extension to the east, housing international passenger processing facilities with nine additional gates and four passenger transfer vehicle loading docks. There is an adjoining five-level car park, for 5,300 cars.

Toronto International has four runways, an air cargo centre used by 80 different agencies, and a yearly throughput of aircraft which generate a total of 243,000 movements — 84,000 of which are private and general aviation.

Below: *The Terminal 2 building at Toronto International is still under development, with the Stage Three extension due for completion at the end of 1978. This will constitute a terminal extension with airbridges at the eastern end (lower left foreground).*

Vienna (Schwechat)   Austria

Location: 10.5 miles SE of Vienna
Elevation: 600ft (183m)
Runways in use: 2
12/30 9,840ft × 150ft (3,000m × 45m)
16/34 11,811ft × 150ft (3,600m × 45m)
Airport area: 2,346 acres
Passengers handled in 1977: 2,578,020
Total air transport movements in 1977: 47,299
Cargo handled in 1977: 37,192 tons

Vienna was amongst the first capitals in Europe to
have regular air transport services, in the early
1920s, and the present site of Vienna Schwechat
has been developed progressively to present a
comfortable and efficient facility for the 2.5 million
passengers that now use the airport annually. There
are two airports serving Vienna (the other being
Aspern), and Schwechat is the major international
terminal, handling the services of some 27 airlines.
While the facilities and aids have been brought right
up to date, the airport buildings are of older design
and in the traditional architectural mould. Thus
passenger buses are used to take travellers from the
terminal to their aircraft, rather than airbridges, or
even projecting terminal piers.

The airport does have the facility of a railway line
serving it, however, and recent work on the stations
and related tunnels of this railway line has provided
an efficient and impressive link between the airport
and the city. It is now possible for travellers to reach
the airport quickly by way of this line, and also to go
directly to the passenger hall by way of tunnels from
the roadway or car parks built for the airport. An
autobahn runs past the airport, and a recent link road
has been built as a spur from this autobahn to the
terminal kerbside. The passenger is thus fairly well
served at Vienna Schwechat with integrated road
and rail facilities.

The most recent development at the airport has
been the construction of a new runway, which was
begun in 1973 and opened for service in the early
part of 1977. This runway is equipped with bad
weather landing aids and high-speed turn-offs to
further the movements at Schwechat, which are now
running at over 72,000 a year.

*Below: A new runway has recently been opened at
Vienna-Schwechat, to handle bigger and heavier
aircraft.*

Washington (Dulles International)   USA

Location: 27 miles west of Washington DC
Elevation: 313ft (95m)
Runways in use: 3
01L/19R 11,500ft × 150ft (3,505m × 45m)
01R/19L 11,500ft × 150ft (3,505m × 45m)
12/30 10,000ft × 150ft (3,048m × 45m)
Airport area: 10,000 acres
Passengers handled in 1977: 2,867,782
Total aircraft movements in 1977: 186,391
Cargo handled in 1977: 35,352 tons

For one of the world's most beautiful capital cities, it is fitting that Washington DC should have a beautiful airport, and Dulles International is the style of airport which has furthered the remarkable growth of air transport. Named after the former US Secretary of State, John Foster Dulles, the funds for the new airport were allocated in 1957, and construction work put in hand in September 1958. The airport was completed in November 1962 and officially opened before 50,000 spectators on 17 November 1962.

Before this, Washington National Airport had served the Federal capital since the mid-1940s. That airport still serves the region today and handled 13 million passengers in 1977, but Dulles International was created as the prime international airline facility, and the airport is established in that role today, although its traffic development has been disappointing so far and growing very little in the last decade.

Dulles is striking in many ways and its dramatic architecture is matched by impressive statistics. The airport covers twice as much ground as New York International, 10,000 acres, and is two-thirds the size of the city of Manhattan. It has one of the tallest control towers in the world, 193ft, and its construction involved the clearing of 1,200 acres of wooded land. When it was built on a specially selected site at Chantilly, Virginia, 27 miles west of the White House, a special access highway and a 14-mile long expressway had to be built for the sole purpose of providing a rapid connecting link between the airport and the city of Washington.

Below: Dulles International Airport is sited at Chantilly, Virginia, 14 miles from the Federal Capitol.

Overleaf: 27 miles west of the White House, Dulles Airport boasts a control tower of 193ft and the beautiful Saarinen-designed passenger terminal and control building.

Above: *The Booth Plane-Mate mobile lounges are 'second-generation' models of this type of passenger-transporter at Dulles, each carrying up to 150 passengers from the terminal to the aircraft doors, The maximum elevating height is 18.5ft.*

The terminal building was designed by the Finnish-born architect Eero Saarinen, who earned a reputation in air transport circles by his bizarre airport architectural creations. The terminal building rises from a base of approach ramps and has a concourse 600ft long and 150ft wide. There are no columns within the space. The hanging roof is supported by a row of columns 40ft apart on each side of the concourse, 60ft high on the approach side and 60ft high on the airfield side. The piers are likened to two rows of trees between which a continuous roof hammock has been hung. The roof is supported by light suspension bridge cables.

The control tower is similarly striking, and constitutes a concrete shaft rising from an observation platform with the control tower cab placed on top. A sphere surmounting the control tower cab houses airport surface detection radar.

Passenger procedures at Dulles are straightforward, with traffic flow taking place on two levels in the terminal. The carriage of passengers from the terminal to the aircraft was effected in a new and unusual way, however. This involved the use of 'Mobile Lounges', otherwise great upholstered coaches driven by engines at either end. An initial 21 of these mobile lounges was bought for Dulles, each

carrying 102 people. This original fleet has since been enlarged with the introduction of 12 second-generation mobile lounges, known as the Plane-Mate, and which each carry 150 passengers. The Plane-Mates were designed to support the wide-bodied jets, and have a maximum speed of 19mph. As with their forerunners, the vehicles carry passengers directly from the terminal exits to the aircraft cabin doors, their doors mating with the side of the aircraft. The bodies of the vehicles are elevated to the required cabin door height by electrically-driven ball screw jacks. The maximum elevating height is 18.5ft.

Fifteen airlines are currently using Dulles, including three overseas airlines, British Airways, Air France and Aeroflot. Both British Airways and Air France operate daily Concorde services to the airport from London and Paris.

In order to provide airline personnel with extra space for sorting baggage and to give another 50ft at the concourse level for passengers boarding and departing from the mobile lounges, a terminal widening contract, expected to take two years, was begun in mid-1978. This project involves the widening of the terminal along its entire length on the airfield side, and will add approximately 75ft to the terminal's width at the ground level. Amongst other things this construction project will provide a second roadway beneath the terminal to separate incoming and outgoing baggage. Consideration is also being given to the widening of the Dulles terminal on both sides.

Zurich (Kloten)   Switzerland

Location: 6 miles from Zurich
Elevation: 1,414ft (430m)
Runways in use: 3
14/32 10,824ft × 200ft (3,300m × 60m)
16/34 12,136ft × 200ft (3,700m × 60m)
10/28 9,184ft × 200ft (2,800m × 60m)
Airport area: 1,790 acres
Passengers handled in 1977: 7,065,600
Total air transport movements in 1977: 109,200
Cargo handled in 1977: 139,100 tons

In the Swiss airport system Zurich is the most important, serving as it does the country's principal city, and Kloten handles the bulk of the traffic. The airport at Kloten is, in air transport history terms, a young one, for sanction of the scheme for an airport and the necessary funds for its building were approved by the citizens of the Canton of Zurich in May 1946. Construction began that summer, and the west runway was opened on 14 June 1948. In November of the same year the instrument landing runway was opened, whereupon all commercial traffic was transferred from the airfield at Dubendorf to the new Kloten Airport, and Zurich's own airport was in business.

It was clear from the outset that the Canton of Zurich would be the owner and operator of the airport, and this situation prevailed until the semi-public Airport Real Estate Company was created to assume financial responsibility for the construction, maintenance and administration of the airport buildings, in particular the terminal buildings. Today, half of this company's shares are held by the Canton of Zurich together with the municipalities of Zurich, Winterthur and Kloten and the Cantonal Bank of Zurich: the other half are privately held. The airport is run by Zurich Flughafen, the Zurich Airport Authority, while responsibility for air traffic control is held by Radio Suisse Ltd, a private company, operated under Federal supervision.

Since the commencement of operations in 1946, there have been a number of expansion schemes at Kloten, and one of the most important of these was begun in 1958, when the instrument runway was lengthened, the ramp was widened, and the airport lighting system substantially improved. Under this development scheme Swissair's technical base was expanded with the construction of a new hangar and workshop and an additional training school building. Finally, a new passenger terminal extension was made, which resulted in a trebling of surface area for passenger handling.

The next phase was the most important, and the people of the Canton of Zurich gave approval for this airport development programme even before the second stage development work had been completed. The heart of this development programme was the construction of a third runway (14/32) for instrument approaches. Apron extensions were also carried out to provide parking stands for some 45 aircraft. In addition, a new wide-bodied aircraft hangar was built, and a new access system to the airport. This last was most important, and included an underground railway link, between the airport and the city of Zurich. This has been integrated into the country's main east-west railway line.

Most important too, was the construction of a new passenger terminal, Terminal B, a three-storey building with a finger dock. Arrivals, departures and transit levels in this terminal are directly connected to the pier, which has nine docking positions. Terminals A and B are connected by corridors in the domestic and transit areas.

Kloten is now handling over seven million passengers annually, and some 145,000 aircraft movements in total.

Below: *The three-runway system at Zurich, showing the most recent runway, 14/32, at right.*

Index